SHAKESPEARE ON THE COUCH

SHAKESPEARE ON THE COUCH

On behalf of the United Kingdom Council for
Psychotherapy by

Michael Jacobs

KARNAC

First published in 2008 by
Karnac Books Ltd
118 Finchley Road, London NW3 5HT

British Library Cataloguing in Publication Data

A C.I.P. for this book is available from the British Library

ISBN 978 1 85575 454 6

Edited, designed and produced by The Studio Publishing Services Ltd
www.studiopublishingservicesuk.co.uk
e-mail: studio@publishingservices.co.uk

Printed in Great Britain

10 9 8 7 6 5 4 3 2 1

www.karnacbooks.com

CONTENTS

Michael Jacobs was at the University of Leicester for most of his career, first as a counsellor and psychotherapist in the Student Health Service, and then as Director of the Counselling and Psychotherapy programme in the Department of Adult Education. He retired from the university in 2000, and moved with his wife to Swanage, in Dorset. There he has a small independent practice offering therapy and supervision, and he is a visiting professor at Bournemouth University. His teaching these days, apart from lectures and workshops throughout the country, concentrates on a study group in his home town where he and a group of largely non-therapist students engage with psychoanalysis and other forms of expression—such as religious faith, Shakespeare, and, currently, film. It is out of two courses on "Shakespeare on the couch" that this book was developed.

Michael Jacobs is perhaps best known in psychodynamic circles for a number of key texts, used on many training courses: notably, *The Presenting Past* (2006, third edition, Open University Press) and *Psychodynamic Counselling in Action* (2004, third edition, Sage). Other publications include: *The Therapist's Use of Self*, written with John Rowan (2002, Open University Press), part of a major international series Michael edited titled *Core Concepts in Therapy*; and *Illusion—A Psychodynamic Interpretation of Thinking and Belief* (2000, Whurr/Wiley). His next book, *Our Desire of Unrest*, will be published by Karnac and consists of papers and lectures that trace his own questioning approach to various psychotherapeutic issues.

He is a UKCP registered psychotherapist, Vice-Chair of the Universities Psychotherapy and Counselling Association, and a Fellow of the British Association for Counselling and Psychotherapy.

PROLOGUE

One of my pastimes has been (since it is well nigh complete now) collecting first editions of the works of J. I. M. Stewart, better known perhaps as the detective novel writer Michael Innes. I am fortunate to have found and purchased every book he wrote, including some from his own library. Stewart was an academic specializing in twentieth-century literature, although after editing Montaigne's essays, the first book of his own was the first of many featuring his detective John Appleby. In the 1950s he started to write novels under his own name; and as an academic he published several books on early twentieth century English novelists.

Like his friend, Auden, Stewart was interested in Freud's theories, and indeed in many of his fictional works there are witty references to psychology of one form or another, mainly of the "depth" kind. Reading Ernest Jones on Hamlet inspired Stewart to write one of several radio plays, where he imagined a Freudian doctor treating Hamlet. As a result of this play being broadcast there was a brief correspondence with Jones, including a gift by Jones to Stewart, inscribed by him, of *Hamlet and Oedipus* (1949), the actual copy now being in my possession. Stewart also reviewed all three volumes of Jones' monumental biography of Freud, and perhaps as a result was asked to deliver the first Ernest Jones Memorial Lecture for the British Psychoanalytical Society—a lecture that he noted, and I have verified since, seems to have disappeared from the Institute's archives, so we have no record of what Stewart said.

One of his academic texts is a book called *Character and Motive in Shakespeare* (1949), in which Stewart argues against those literary critics who had dismissed many of Shakespeare's most important characters as mere fictions, and as behaving and reacting in a manner that is unreal. Stewart draws considerably upon Freud and psychoanalytic ideas to support his argument that, if we look below the surface, we find that many of these characters in fact portray the very traits that Freud's patients would also show. His arguments are virtually straight down the line Freudian—there is no suggestion that he had read more widely in psychoanalytic literature. But his book started me thinking.

Fifty years later Harold Bloom published a huge volume titled *Shakespeare: The Invention of the Human* (1999). Bloom, like Stewart, is a literary critic first and foremost, but unlike Stewart is no admirer of Freud. Nevertheless, he treats many of the same characters in a similar way, showing just how contemporary they are in their reactions and relationships.

The two texts together prompted me to look further into this interesting argument. How real are Shakespeare's characters? How might a therapist understand them if they were "on the couch"?

As Chapter One makes clear, there have been many analysts who have tried their hand at interpreting the major characters in the Shakespeare canon. So here was even more food for thought, and, when given the opportunity to take a class for the Workers Educational Association in my home town of Swanage, a ready subject presented itself. Swanage WEA members are usually no longer workers as such, but a group of bright, mainly retired men and women who shared my enthusiasm for the subject, and were already familiar with some psychoanalytic ideas from past courses. They enjoyed first one course, and then a second, on "Shakespeare on the Couch".

We had the advantage, which the reader unfortunately does not have, of being able to view clips of productions available on video and DVD, in conjunction with the material here. This added much to the appreciation of the subject, especially when some of the actors themselves, in the extra tracks on DVDs, were able to speak of their understanding of their roles. I have none the less included references to all the productions we used, listed in the bibliography under the name of the play itself.

There was a huge amount of material to draw upon—articles from journals, the two texts which had inspired me to look deeper, and other references which are included in the text that follows. Discussions on how some of these situations play out in today's families were an important element of the course, a feature that prompted looking at ourselves as well. That aspect has not been included in this book, although the purpose in writing it is to encourage the reader, whether or not a therapist or a client, to reflect upon the way in which either Shakespeare's characters, or their interpreters, or both, may promote self-knowledge as well as understanding of others.

It is appropriate, then, to thank the participants on the two courses in Swanage for their enthusiastic response to the subject, their contributions to further reflection, and their encouragement for what they enjoyed in person to be published so others may also enjoy what they appreciated at one remove.

Michael Jacobs
Swanage
September 2007

CHAPTER ONE

The qualities of people

P sychoanalysis has developed an enduring interest in literature, just as literary criticism has not been averse to drawing
upon various possibilities thrown up by psychoanalysis.
Perhaps this is not surprising when Freud wrote of his own case
histories: 'It still strikes me myself as strange that the case histories
I write should read like short stories and that, as one might say, they
lack the serious stamp of science' (Freud & Breuer, 1895d, p. 160).
The richness of his associations appears to show sheer enjoyment
and fascination as he explored the imagery and relationships in a
once popular novel, Jensen's *Gradiva* (1907a). Other essays of his
use literary figures, sometimes through his wish to protect the
confidentiality of his patients (e.g., 1916d), sometimes because the
figures themselves lead to interesting speculation (e.g., 1913f).
Shakespeare's characters, as well as indeed the identity of
Shakespeare himself (a mistaken hypothesis in Freud's case)
also feature strongly in some of his essays, as well as in his major
works, such as *The Interpretation of Dreams* (1900a). The chapters
that follow demonstrate how often Shakespeare's characters have
either been the basis of psychoanalytic study in themselves, or have
informed or been informed by the case work of many analysts. Two
articles (Greenberg & Rothenberg, 1974; Willbern, 1978), which list

references to Shakespeare's plays, principally in psychoanalytic literature, provide respectively details of 318 and 316 articles or books; and Levey (1993) lists 403 more that have been published since the appearance of those bibliographies.

Inevitably most of these articles are vehicles for the authors' views, rather than accurate representations of what Shakespeare may or may not have intended. How could they be otherwise? Analysing those who cannot respond for themselves is inevitably speculative, although not illegitimate, as long as it provokes ideas in the reader. At times some authors appear to stretch the text too far, making interpretations that milk the material dry to provide evidence of their particular psychoanalytic theory, or for their application of a more general psychoanalytic theory. Symons (1928), for example, draws all manner of wild and unprovable conclusions from the graveyard scene in *Hamlet*, interpreting practically every word and symbol as referring to Shakespeare's issues with his own father. Freud, too, was tempted on occasion to make an excursion into literary criticism, looking at possible issues in Shakespeare himself. These are hard theories to sustain. That is definitely not one of the purposes of this book, even if the title might lead the unsuspecting reader to think this is an imaginative case study of Shakespeare himself, as if he were lying upon the author's couch.

While psychoanalytic writing is the richest of the psychologies in interpreting Shakespeare's characters, suggesting helpful parallels to contemporary psychological ideas, it is not the only one. Peter Murray, an American professor of English, discovers in that most classical of behavioural psychologists, B. F. Skinner, ways of understanding some of Shakespeare's characters; and the title of his book, *Shakespeare's Imagined Persons* (1996), perhaps allows not just for Shakespeare's imagination, but also for the imagination of the contemporary reader, using those characters as springboards to self reflection. That is more to the purpose of these chapters, too.

What are remarkable are the parallels between the figures that most intensely occupy the minds of analysts and critics alike. For example, Harold Bloom (1999) (a frank anti-Freudian), writing from a literary perspective, highlights Hamlet, Falstaff, and Rosalind in *As You Like It* as the most rounded of all Shakespeare's characters. Murray does the same; and names that appear in Stewart's Freudian interpretations in *Character and Motive in Shakespeare* (1949)

again loom out of the page in Murray's behavioural reflections—
Othello and Leontes, for example.

But if Bloom is sceptical of much Freudian interpretation, he
demonstrates a similar fascination with character. He believes, for
example, that Falstaff and Hamlet, above all of Shakespeare's characters, are the invention, that is the finding or the finding out, of the
human, and the "inauguration of personality as we have come to
recognize it" (Bloom, 1999, p. 4). Indeed, Bloom goes so far as to say
that personality, in the sense we understand it, is "a Shakespearean
invention" (ibid.). Like Stewart before him, he refers to those who
dispute such a view. He writes that "I never know how to take the
assurances (and remonstrances) I receive from Shakespeare's
current critics, who tell me that Falstaff, Hamlet, Rosalind, Cleopatra, and Iago are roles for actors and actresses, but not 'real
people'"(ibid., pp. 14–15). Bloom could not disagree more. He
recalls as a child seeing Ralph Richardson play Falstaff, and there-
after never being able to see Richardson on stage or screen without
identifying him with Falstaff, for all Richardson's extraordinary
genius. The role takes over: Falstaff is more real than the actor who
plays him. So, says Bloom, in meeting Shakespeare's characters, we
know something not about them, but about ourselves:

> If your Falstaff is a roistering coward, a wastrel confidence man, an
> uncourted jester to Prince Hal, well, then, we know something of
> you, but we know no more about Falstaff. If your Cleopatra is an
> ageing whore, and her Antony a would-be Alexander in his dotage,
> then we know a touch more about you and rather less about them
> than we should. Hamlet's players hold the mirror up to nature.
> [Bloom, 1999, p. 15]

Bloom concludes his introductory chapter with the observation
that there are two contradictory ways of accounting for Shakespeare's greatness (ibid., p. 16). One is that his language is superb, his
poetry wonderful, and that he has contributed so much to the
development of our English language. The other is to say that what
makes him supreme is that he has represented the universe of
fact—not poetry - better than anyone before him or since. So when
Broadmoor patients and staff comment on seeing the Royal
Shakespeare Company perform Shakespeare in their hospital, it is

clear that they appreciate what Shakespeare means, not what he writes:

> "I didn't understand the words, but I understood the feelings"; "I didn't understand many of the words they were using, and I found the story hard to follow, but I understood every bit of emotion"; "You felt emotion—and the play was written 400 years ago . . . The horror you may imagine most people would feel on discovering madness in a loved relative was wonderfully portrayed:"; "I am amazed that that far back he could understand . . . In King Lear's part for example, it was clear that he was more than emotionally upset. He became deranged. All those centuries ago, were they aware of derangement?" [Cox, 1992, pp. 149, 144, 151]

Bloom appears to relegate actors to a lesser role than the words they speak, as if the character takes them over. Yet they, too, bring to the play their own understanding of what it is to be human, and in some cases have spoken, as later chapters will show, of their research into the psychology of the characters they are about to play. There are very different interpretations of the same character, depending upon who is playing the role, and who is directing the play. The actors may also be informed by Freud, if often indirectly, since Freudian ideas have soaked into Western culture, whether or not they are right. Bloom writes that Shakespeare, "rather than his involuntary follower Freud, is our psychologist" (1999, p. 17), but to argue precedent is to risk losing the insights of those who follow. So the actors are essential, too, if the play is, in Hamlet's words, to "catch the conscience"; in his case of the king, in theatre the conscience of the audience. Poor actors will obscure rather than reveal Shakespeare's insight, as Hamlet warns the players in his instructions to them before the play, which he hopes will reveal the truth about the murder of his father: "It offends me to the soul to hear a robustious periwig-pated fellow tear a passion to tatters, to very rags, to split the ears of the groundlings" (*Hamlet*, 3(ii): 8–11).

Actors and directors are also informed by present-day culture, and the setting might be informed by contemporary circumstances: e.g., the National Theatre's production of *Henry V*, for instance, at the time Blair was taking the UK to war in Iraq, where the parallels were emphasized. James Shapiro, in his book *1599* (2005) has shown convincingly how Shakespeare, too, was influenced in writing some of his plays by events at the time. While *Henry V*, performed first in 1599, was not "a political manifesto" it was nevertheless "a going-to-war play" relevant to the Earl of Essex's imminent departure to campaign in Ireland (*ibid.*, p. 104).

Shakespeare must be acted, and seen, not just read as we might a novel or poetry. This poses a problem for this book, since to illustrate the subtleties of interpretation the reader needs to be able to see the characters live, as portrayed by the actors. Theatre, from Greek drama onwards, is partly a type of catharsis, a way of purging the emotions through arousing them in the audience set at a slight distance from the stage. Freud suggested that when we watch Oedipus,

> the Greek legend seizes upon a compulsion which everyone recognizes because he senses its existence within himself. Everyone in the audience was once a budding Oedipus in fantasy and each recoils in horror from the dream fulfilment here represented into reality [Masson, 1985, p. 272]

Freud goes on in the next paragraph of this letter to his colleague Fliess to refer to Hamlet, initiating a theory that Hamlet is a repressed version of Oedipus, with the same oedipal issues; and that it is this that makes the play so powerful, because the members of the audience similarly struggle with these universal desires (see also Freud, 1914b, pp. 212).

It is not necessary to accept Freud's interpretation of Hamlet's struggles to understand his argument, that what the spectator witnesses in great drama are his or her own intra- and interpersonal issues. What is more relevant here, to put it crudely, is how theatre, as an art form, works. Why does a particular play appeal to us? Both Freud and another psychoanalytic commentator on art, Ernst Kris, suggest that art moves two parts of us—the id and the ego (this is, of course, to use Freud's simple tripartite model of personality). The id's drives—love, hate, incest, murder, jealousy, etc.—are the stuff of drama. Acted out on stage, the id is given some form of expression, which makes for some vicarious satisfaction in the audience. We may well also admire the form and structure of the drama, the way it is written, in Shakespeare's case the poetry and the reworking of his sources into a more satisfying plot. It is this, according to Freud and Kris, that appeals to the ego.

But the analyst Frattaroli (1990) proposes another theory of aesthetic response, rather than Freud's rather limited model. He observes, following Waelder, that there is in Freud's model of personality a third element, the superego, usually understood in Freudian terms as a critical, somewhat cruel voice in us, fighting the id-drives, influencing the ego. Waelder gives a different twist to the superego:

> It is the element by which man . . . goes beyond himself, taking himself as an object, whether acting in a punishing aggressive way, or lovingly caring, or finally, being disinterestedly objective, as in self-observation and the ability to depart from his own point of view. Here also belongs the ability to see a garden as a garden, regardless of the place from which one observes it at the moment. Here belongs the faculty of not only experiencing the world around one in its momentary relationship to one's drives and interests, but also of recognizing its existence apart from one's own ego. [1930, pp. 82–83]

Frattaroli therefore suggests that there is a third element in our appreciation of a play. It is not the superego solely as the conscience, which, for example, Hamlet wishes to catch in his stepfather through staging a play about murder (*Hamlet*, 2(ii): 601). That is only one way in which members of the audience are encouraged to reflect upon themselves. In this reflective function the superego need not be judgemental in any cruel, upbraiding sense (such as a "preaching" play might hope to stir), but judgemental more in the sense of reflecting, or weighing up, similar to Freud's concept of the ego-ideal (a twin concept of the superego), which is that part of us that strives for something better or more fulfilling. It is, as Frattaroli puts it, "the ability to step back and take a look at oneself from an imaginary observation point" (1990, p. 273). The primary purpose of art is not therefore to discharge (the id-drives), but to promote awareness, to make us more aware of ourselves, of the world about us, and of others. Hamlet puts it this way to the players, and is naturally quoted by Frattaroli, that the purpose of drama "is to hold as 'twere the mirror up to nature; to show virtue her feature, scorn her own image, and the very age and body of the time his form and pressure" (*Hamlet*, 3(ii): 21–24).

Frattaroli (1990, pp. 275–276) observes that Freud equates art with dreaming—"the imaginary satisfactions of unconscious wishes" (1925a, p. 249). Frattaroli believes that art is more like science than dreaming:

> Art has the same purpose as science, to understand, represent and communicate experience. The instinctual wish-fulfilling purpose of dreaming is fundamentally different. To the extent that the artist is aiming at wish-fulfilment, he is creating not art but entertainment. [1990, p. 276]

What happens then if we begin to see the play *Hamlet* in this light? It is not just about the struggle with the id-drives, in this instance incest and murder. It is not just a beautifully crafted play, one that appeals to the ego. It is also a play about a person struggling with self-reflection, which echoes our own struggles with self-reflection.

This is an important idea for this book, too. Shakespeare's major characters in many instances suggest possibilities for self-reflection. They are "human", "real", imagined perhaps, but "imagined persons". Shakespeare draws upon observation and a depth of insight that prefigures, and even overshadows, later attempts to reflect upon the nature of personality, and of human relationships. What psychologists have added to this are names and labels and theories that attempt to explain the wellsprings of emotions, actions, and relationships.

Yet there is an assumption already that needs to be questioned. Do Shakespeare's characters, penned around four hundred years ago, really inform us about "the qualities of people" today? The appeal of Shakespeare's plays appears to answer that question, if Frattaroli's theory of art is correct. Yet, if that is the case, what of the appeal of novels and films, for example, which contain a large amount of fantasy, where the characters there are either nothing like us, or get into and out of situations that are far-fetched. Are these examples of what Frattaroli calls "entertainment" rather than art? Are such works pure escapism—stories that wing us away from our human condition and indulge our fantasies of what life might be like if only we were not so bound by our limitations?

The same argument has been made that Shakespeare similarly wrote for his audience, a large number of whom were either young nobles eager for a slice of life, or the groundlings standing in the well of the theatre and looking for blood, as Stoppard's Player King in *Rosencrantz and Guildenstern Are Dead* describes theatre and actors:

Player: We're more of the love, blood and rhetoric school. Well, we can do you blood and love without the rhetoric, and we can do you blood and rhetoric without the love, and we can do all three, concurrent and consecutive; but we can't give you rhetoric without the blood. Blood is compulsory. They're all blood, you see.

Guildenstern: Is that what people want?

Player: It's what we do. [Stoppard, 1990]

The German critic Rümelin, writing in the nineteenth century about Shakespeare's audience, concentrated more upon the young nobles, who wanted "poetry, surprising and abundant action, stories of amatory intrigue such as occupied their own extensive leisure; they welcomed extravagance and tolerated improbability and contraction; they were uninterested in psychological realism" (Stewart, 1949, p.12). This type of thinking also underlies Robert Bridges' essay on 'The influence of the audience on Shakespeare's drama' first printed in 1907 (*ibid.*, pp. 13ff). Scenes such as the murder of McDuff's child in *Macbeth*, or the blinding of Gloucester in *King Lear* were, according to such theories, pandering to the coarseness of Shakespeare's audience, the same audience that would have revelled in bear-baiting, cock-fighting, and other bloody sports. Robert Bridges concludes his 1907 essay with these remarkable words: "Shakespeare should not be put into the hands of the young without the warning that the foolish things in his plays were written to please the foolish, the filthy for the filthy, and the brutal for the brutal" (cited by Stewart, 1949, p. 16).

Such critics are in the minority, and Stewart's *Character and Motive in Shakespeare* expressly counters such views. The influence of psychoanalytic ideas is evident in his writing (as it is, indeed, in his detective genre written under the name Michael Innes). It was that slim volume that prompted the present writer to further study of Shakespeare's characters as understood by various psychoanalytic writers. Such a realistic view is not new, as Stewart shows in opening his study with a quotation from Samuel Johnson:

> [Shakespeare] had looked with great attention on the scenes of nature; but his chief skill was in human actions passions and habits . . . his works may be considered as a map of life, a faithful miniature of human transactions . . . the love and hatred, the hopes and fears of his chief personages are such as are common to other human beings. [cited in Stewart, 1949, p. 1]

Shakespeare's characters provide a rich resource for psychologists, mainly of the psychoanalytic persuasion, to play with their interpretations. Some of these the reader will find fascinating; others too strained. Whatever the response, and this will vary from reader to reader, this approach has the potentiality to throw light on the reality of the situations that Shakespeare describes—in other words, that they are not just written for dramatic effect. Sometimes psychoanalytic ideas demonstrate how the relationships between characters on the stage in certain ways reflect the internal world of some of those who have graced the contemporary couch, and they may in some way reflect upon the psyche of the reader too. Even if psychoanalytic interpretations are no more than the authors' own projections on to the material, they are informative for all that, if not of Shakespeare or of his characters, at least of psychoanalytic thinking. That thinking must, however, always be measured against the reader's experience if it is to have any value.

Drawing upon what is actually a vast literature in psychoanalytic journals, either interpreting the characters themselves, or alluding to the characters in the course of other topics, this book then demonstrates how psychoanalytic and literary interpretations not only throw possible light upon some of Shakespeare's most notable characters, but also upon present psychological states, upon current human relationships, and upon contemporary theories. Without claiming any literary critical validity, and certainly not claiming to analyse Shakespeare himself, the following chapters seek to engage the imagination and thinking of the reader. The validity in this approach can only be realized when psychoanalytic criticism "rings bells" in the reader and enables the reader to consider aspects of his or her own personality, thoughts, fantasies and behaviours.

Are these characters real? Do they reflect our own experiences, or the experiences of those we know among our friends, family, patients, and clients? And, in addition to speaking of what we already know, do they and their interpreters help us understand "the qualities of people" (*Antony and Cleopatra*, 1(i): 55)? In the chapters that follow, let the characters speak, the actors embody, and the psychologists interpret to see what comes of inviting Shakespeare's creations to lie on the couch.

CHAPTER TWO

Much deceived: Leontes and Othello

L eontes, in *The Winter's Tale*, and Othello have this in common. Both become intensely jealous, with disastrous results
for themselves as well as for their wives. In Leontes' case this
jealousy appears to spring from nowhere; and with Othello he is set
up by his trusted companion Iago. But can we really believe in the
intensity of their jealousy? These two characters provide dramatic
examples of the debate referred to in Chapter One: do they accu-
rately represent states of mind that contemporary men and women
feel? Are there relationships such as theirs where innocent partners
are psychologically or literally destroyed? Or does Shakespeare
create these situations to titillate and entertain? More generously,
does he exaggerate in order to draw attention to possibilities otherwise only faintly acknowledged within us?

The first act of *The Winter's Tale* is all the more remarkable
because, within one hundred lines, and on very little pretext,
Leontes appears to snap, turning on his heavily pregnant wife Hermione; and within a few lines he is seething with jealousy, all
because Hermione has persuaded his boyhood friend Polixenes to
stay on at court a little longer.

Matters of state had separated Leontes and Polixenes in their childhood, and although they regularly wrote to each other, when the play opens they had only recently met again, when Polixenes, King of Bohemia, visited Leontes' court in Sicily. This visit is coming to an end and Leontes begs Polixenes to stay longer. Polixenes says that he cannot; but then Hermione, Leontes' wife, persuades Polixenes to stay a little longer. It is this that, almost out of the blue, suddenly fires up Leontes' jealousy.

The 1999 production by the Royal Shakespeare Company at the Barbican Theatre, London, with Sir Antony Sher and Alexandra Galbraith as Leontes and Hermione, powerfully demonstrates the suddenness and intensity of this jealousy. As the curtain rises Leontes and Polixenes approach the audience, identically dressed in their regal robes, almost as if they are twins; and, even as they remove these ceremonial garments, there is an electricity between them. Leontes touches Polixenes, steers him towards Hermione, and the friendship between the two men is obvious. Additionally, as he says in an interview on the role, Sher indicates that they played the two as also competitive, with Polixenes the more handsome and sexy. Leontes leaves Hermione and Polixenes together as he looks at state papers at his desk, and our attention turns to this couple. Hermione teases Polixenes: "You shall, not go . . . my prisoner or my guest". She puts on music and sedately dances with him, drawing out of Polixenes the story of his boyhood friendship with Leontes. They were "as twinn'd lambs that did frisk i' the sun". He paints a picture of their innocence together as boys.

When Leontes looks up from his papers, he asks Hermione whether Polixenes is won over. No sooner does Hermione say that he will stay, than Leontes immediately responds somewhat testily, "At my request he would not". He already shows a hint of bitterness that she has succeeded where he could not. For herself, Hermione looks innocently pleased, but Leontes quickly taxes her sarcastically with an event long ago, when she kept him waiting three months before accepting his proposal of marriage. As Sher comments, this sleight has been festering in his head ever since. Leontes appears to feign pleasure at Polixenes' decision to stay, and, as Hermione and Polixenes take up their dance in the background, Leontes explodes with "Too hot, too hot", anxiety written all over him. He continues to mull over this new situation, as he imagines it to be, as Hermione and Polixenes chat together in the background. But from this point onwards everything that happens simply confirms Leonte's suspicion of something going on between the two of them. Hermione's baby kicks in the womb and she expresses some pain. Leontes appears to interpret this as an erotic sigh. He aims a playful blow at Polixenes, and then himself joins their hands together, sending them into the garden. But as soon as they leave he once more explodes, clearly, in Sher's words, "a sick man, an ill man". He aggressively points at his six-year-old son Maimonides, sending him off to play, spitting out "Thy mother plays"; and he sniffs at the stole she has left behind as if he tries to scent her infidelity.

Yet, if this appears convincing on stage, Robert Bridges maintains that Leontes' jealousy is "senseless", while other critics call it "extravagant" or "an impossible improbability"—Quiller Couch suggests that Shakespeare was in a hurry to get the action going at the start of the play (see Stewart, 1949, p. 30). Others think that though the outburst is a possibility, it is only to be found in those whose behaviour is bizarre, such as we might find in mental illness. But could it be, not that Shakespeare is playing a theatrical trick, or raising the borders of psychological possibility as Stewart puts it (*ibid.*, p. 31), but rather that he has portrayed here a little recognized impulse in many people's minds? Instead of cheap theatre this is what might be familiar in what Stewart calls "a rather expensive type of consulting room" (*ibid.*, p. 33).

Stewart has Freud in mind here, but Sir Antony Sher also found an explanation for this sudden outburst through consulting various experts, including one whom he mentioned by name, Professor Maria Ron, now Professor of Neuropsychiatry at the Institute of Neurology, University College, London. She named the condition for Sher as morbid jealousy, saying that it was an example of mental illness, although not the behaviour of a psychopath. It particularly affects men in their forties and can lead to complete unreasonableness and violence, both of which are demonstrated in Sher's portrayal of Leontes. Professor Ron might have pointed Sher (as she did this author) to the seminal paper by Shepherd (1961). Morbid jealousy is sometimes called the Othello syndrome, although, as I observe below, there is a crucial difference between the onset of the jealousy in Leontes and that which developed over time in Othello.

A feature of morbid jealousy is that "individuals interpret conclusive evidence of infidelity from irrelevant occurrences, refuse to change their beliefs even in the face of conflicting information, and tend to accuse the partner of infidelity with many others" (Kingham & Gordon, 2004, p. 208). Kingham and Gordon's paper is a useful summary, from a psychiatric perspective, of the different ways in which morbid jealousy can be associated with other conditions such as obsessive-compulsive disorder, borderline personality, psychosis, alcoholism, and sexual dysfunction. There is also a link to Parkinson's Disease. The paper outlines the different theories that attempt to explain its genesis, with there being no apparent position that is any more convincing than another. The authors distinguish normal jealousy from morbid jealousy, and summarize the risks involved in the more serious condition: "Morbid jealousy has the potential to cause enormous distress to both partners within a relationship and to their family. It carries with it a risk of serious violence and suicide" (*ibid.*, p. 214). This is clearly the case with Othello, who murders his wife; and Sher's portrayal of Leontes demonstrates that character's potential for violence in the way he manhandles his still pregnant wife in the "trial" scene, throwing her violently to the ground.

Sher was obviously helped to verify Leontes' mental state, a condition which some critics have said stretches credulity. He does not mention, as is to be expected, any theory of its cause, concentrating instead on making his character's words and actions believable. Kingham and Gordon mention several possibilities, ranging from attachment theory (with insecure attachment as the predisposing cause), to cognitive theory, whereby the individual reinforces a precipitating event with faulty assumptions, and even oedipal issues (such as seeing the mother engaged in extra-marital activity), although in this instance to be treated with cognitive therapy.

Stewart, writing more than half a century before all this, draws upon Freud for a fuller explanation of the causes of what Freud termed delusional jealousy. He quotes Freud at length (Stewart, 1949, pp. 33–35) in stating that there are three layers of jealousy (1) competitive or normal jealousy; (2) projected jealousy; and (3) delusional jealousy.

Kingham and Gordon (2004) cite a study distinguishing normal from obsessional jealousy (Marazziti, Di Nasso, & Masala, 2003).

They found that in the more extreme form a greater amount of time is occupied with jealous concerns, with more difficulty putting such concerns out of mind; that there is greater impairment of the relationship and greater limitation of the partner's freedom; and that there is more checking on the partner's behaviour.

Freud appears to accept that competitive or normal jealousy is a part of ordinary relationships. His second layer moves into explanation, that jealous thoughts are projections by a man or a woman on to their partner, whereas in truth it is the jealous person who either has been unfaithful, or has experienced impulses towards unfaithfulness, and has either repressed or forgotten such desires. "It is a matter of everyday experience that fidelity, especially that degree of it required in marriage is only maintained in the face of continual temptation", writes Freud (1924, pp. 232f). Instead of owning the thought or the memory of infidelity, in this second layer infidelity is projected on to the partner. "The person can justify himself with the reflection that the other is probably not much better than he is himself" (*ibid*.). Indeed, we might add, the thought might even be: "He or she is worse than me, because I choose to forget or repress my own desires, and only see them in him (or her)".

Delusional jealousy is even stronger—and, according to Freud, has its origin again in repressed impulses towards unfaithfulness, but in this case where the same sex is the object of the desires. Delusional jealousy is a form of paranoia, an attempt at a defence against a homosexual impulse where it might be said, in a type of unconscious dialogue: "Indeed, *I* do not love him, *she* loves him". While it is important not to get caught on the homophobic bias of some psychoanalytic thought, it is important to recognize that what Freud really draws attention to here is not homosexuality as such, but *repressed* homosexual desires. It is interesting that from a psychiatric perspective one study describes abnormal jealousy in homosexual patients, admittedly within a special hospital setting (Gordon, Oyebode, & Minne, 1997). Furthermore, the critic Harold Bloom, who normally eschews a Freudian interpretation, comments upon seeing Gielgud in the role of Leontes in 1951, "superbly incarnating the madness of sexual jealousy, while subtly hinting that his paranoia stemmed from too close an identity with Polixenes" (1999, p. 640). Later he goes on to say that "the love between the two pre-adolescent boys seems not to have marked Polixenes, but it may well be the root of Leontes' madness" (1999, p. 641). Bloom remains unsure "whether or not there is repressed homosexuality in Leontes' aberration" (*ibid.*, p. 645). I have already drawn attention to the tactile relationship that Leontes has with Polixenes in Sher's interpretation.

Freud illustrates his theory from a case of a youngish man jealous of his impeccably faithful wife. He would observe the smallest possible indications that might have been unnoticeable to any other person—such as her unintentionally touching the man sitting next to her with her hand, turning too much towards him, and smiling more pleasantly than when she was alone with her husband. Any signs such as these he would note, believing he had interpreted them correctly, and that he was always right about them, and he would see them as confirmation of his jealousy. The cognitive theory of reinforced cognitive assumptions also applies here; and Cicely Berry, the voice director for the 1999 production of *The Winter's Tale*, stresses in an interview how "everything [Leontes] says leads him to the next thought and reinforces his feelings, and reinforces the incredible jealousy he has". Freud writes of his young male patient, "He watched his wife's unconscious mind much more closely and then regarded it as far more important than anyone else would have thought of doing". We might add that the young man monitored his wife's unconscious mind more closely than he observed his own.

Leontes may then fit this pattern. First, there is possibly Freud's second layer of projected jealousy, because the text, Stewart suggests, hints that one of the lords at his court, Camillo, has been Leontes' confidant, and "assistant in covert immoralities" (1949, p. 35). Projected jealousy is much more common than morbid or delusional jealousy. Yet the delusional layer might be seen as well, when, as Hermione and Polixenes dance together (and speak indeed of the two men's youth), there may be a stirring of Leontes' early closeness upon his boyhood friend Polixenes. Therefore, on this interpretation, Leontes projects on to his wife Hermione the desires he has to repudiate in himself. Hermione's relationship to Polixenes, as portrayed by Alexandra Galbraith in the same production, clearly contains an element of flirtation, but this is an element in relationships which Freud suggests is sanctioned in society; in other words, we use a form of social flirtation to safeguard against actual infidelity. By expressing something of our desires light-heart-edly we discharge them in a type of fantasy relationship, which we do not expect to be acted upon. Sometimes, of course, flirtation does lead to acting out, but more often than not it is a socially acceptable way, as long as it is not over played, of diverting infidelity rather than of promoting it.

The destructiveness of morbid jealousy, to which Kingham and Gordon (2004) devote a large part of their article (under the head-ing "Risk to others"), is clearly seen in the manner in which Leontes accuses his wife of bearing Polixenes' child: "Polixenes has made thee swell thus" (Act 2(i): 60–61), even though it would appear Polixenes might not even have been at the court at the child's conception. Leontes is violent in language and in action towards Hermione, and condemns her to prison.

There are yet other dimensions that psychoanalytic commentary has considered, expanding the possible explanations of Leontes' intense jealousy. In a chapter on *The Winter's Tale* in his study of narcissism and marriage, Fisher (1999) fastens upon Leontes' conviction that his friend Polixenes, his guest for nine months, has betrayed him with Hermione, his queen, and that the baby she carries is not his. Fisher draws out the family tensions between the couple and their small son Mamillius. Fisher suggests a new term, "Leontean", for the jealousy and rivalry of a parent towards his (or, less likely, her) child, in this instance as yet unborn. Sher's portrayal of Leontes suggests some tension towards his son too, in the way he speaks to the wheelchair-bound Mamillius

Fisher's chapter about *The Winter's Tale* is entitled "Marriage and re-marriage" and his book *The Uninvited Guest*. There are three variations on this theme. First, a therapist working with a couple may be in one way an uninvited intruder into the relationship, someone who communicates difficult truths, as Hermione's lady-in-waiting does in *The Winter's Tale*. Second, Polixenes outstays his welcome as a guest (even though it is at Leontes' bidding initially). Last, and perhaps most significantly, the unborn baby is "unin-vited" once Leontes becomes insanely suspicious. In the Sher portrayal, his violent temper stops short of kicking Alexandra Galbraith's Hermione in her swollen abdomen, but he is right on the edge of such brutality. As the play proceeds we witness the destruction of this family. Mamillius dies of grief when his mother is so cruelly accused. We imagine that Hermione dies after giving birth to a baby girl, Perdita, "the lost one", who, as Boswell observes in her review of Fisher's book, represents a variation on the Oedipus myth where she is left to die. But, like Oedipus, she is rescued and later falls in love with the son of Polixenes. Fisher interprets Leontes' final defence of this young couple's marriage as reparative, allowing their children their right to life and to their own sexual union (see Boswell, 2000).

Discovering Perdita as an adult—lost then found—initiates the restoration of the relationship between Leontes and Hermione. He had thought her dead, too, but she now is returned to him through a theatrical device that does not (and perhaps was not intended to) ring true. But some commentators have drawn more attention to the theme of the father–daughter relationship, and that it is a key feature in Shakespeare's last four plays—*Pericles*, *Cymbeline*, *The Winter's Tale*, and *The Tempest*. It is certainly a powerful feature, as subsequent chapters show, in Shylock, Lear, and Prospero.

The finale of *The Winter's Tale* is indeed contrived and virtually unbelievable. But its start is not, despite the suddenness of Leontes' change of mood. What appears shocking to Leontes' court, as well as to the audience, is not an arbitrary device to get the play going, to inject some spice into the plot. The plot follows a psychological pattern that is real enough. Greg Doran, director of the production that is drawn upon here, says in an interview on the DVD of the production that this play, more than anything else in literature, "explores sexual obsession with acute observation, psychological depth and realism" (*The Winter's Tale*, 1999). Shakespeare, far from "sacrificing nature to a cheap effect" (Stewart, 1949, p. 36) pene-trates to human nature.

But if this morbid jealousy is sometimes called the Othello syn-drome, there are differences between Leontes and Othello. Leontes' jealousy appears spontaneously, apparently out of nowhere, whereas Othello's jealousy is first planted, and then nurtured, by his lieutenant Iago. But those critics who see Leontes as a fiction, also see in Othello and Iago artistic creations who hold no real credibility.

A reminder of the plot of *Othello* immediately reveals some of these differences between the onset of jealousy in Leontes and its onset in Othello. The play opens with Iago, Othello's ensign, complaining about being passed over for promotion. Othello has instead made Michael Cassio his lieutenant. Iago is out for revenge, which will pull down both Othello and Cassio. He stirs up trouble in the house of Desdemona's father, by revealing that Desdemona has gone to Othello without her father's permission. Othello appears to have won Desdemona's heart with tales of his gallantry: "She lov'd me for the danger I had passed" (1(iii): 167). This is an early hint of an idealized relationship, on both their parts—and it is possible that the greater the idealization, the greater the fall from it when the first signs of the commonplace emerge. Yet, even at this early stage, her father warns Othello, not unreasonably, that "she has deceiv'd her father, and may thee" (1(iii): 293). Iago remembers this and later reminds Othello: "She did deceive her father" (3(iii): 210). This might be said to be a not altogether unreasonable doubt.

Othello is employed by the Venetians to fight against the Turks, and he does indeed win a triumphant battle over them. He arrives in Cyprus, where his newly-wed wife Desdemona has preceded him. Iago now works his poisonous ploys in earnest, setting Cassio up to be dismissed from office, and then fixing it so that Desdemona pleads for Cassio's reinstatement. He sows doubts in Othello's mind about Desdemona's fidelity. Othello's thoughts are therefore not self-generated, even though there must be fertile ground in which the seed can take root. Iago's scheme is further advanced by planting on Cassio a handkerchief dropped by Desdemona. This is the clue that convinces Othello of her unfaithfulness, and his suspicion certainly increases in magnitude, so that it now becomes as strong as that shown by Leontes. Nevertheless, the cleverness of the writing lies in the subtle ways in which Iago fosters Othello's doubts, using what might be called today paradoxical interventions as well as carefully timed and worded hints: "Beware, my lord, of jealousy; / It is the green-ey'd monster which doth mock / The meat it feeds on" (3(iii): 169–170). We might contrast Camillo's sincere attempts to dissuade Leontes from his accusations against Hermione. Iago is trusted by Othello—"a man he is of honesty and trust" (1(iii): 284)—so that it is not surprising that Othello is seduced into suspicion and jealousy. Furthermore, "Iago everywhere passes as honest" (Stewart, 1949, p. 103). He is equally convincing to the gullible Rodorigo, who is in love with Desdemona and continually follows Iago's advice, even though the evidence flies in the face of believing it; and to Cassio, whom he draws unwittingly into his plot against Othello and Desdemona. Only Iago's wife Emilia seems to see through him, describing him at one point as "My wayward husband" (3(iii): 296).

Of course, Othello's jealousy builds to a point far beyond that of Leontes, since he murders his wife, despite her vehement protestations of innocence. (Leontes does not go quite so far, although his treatment of Hermione might have broken her spirit.) Only when Iago is unmasked does Othello realize the enormity of what he has been led to believe and act upon. At the same time there are some obvious similarities to the story of Leontes. Othello is not prepared to accept any of Desdemona's protestations of innocence—which are certainly forcefully made in, for example, Imogen Stubbs' Desdemona in the Trevor Nunn production on DVD (2003). Furthermore, Emilia, Desdemona's maid, could be describing Leontes as much as Othello when she says, in response to Desdemona's cry of innocence:

> But jealous souls will not be answer'd so;
> They are not ever jealous for the cause,
> But jealous for they are jealous. 'Tis a monster
> Begot upon it self, born of it self. [3(iv): 160–163]

The critics who say that this stretches credulity argue that for a triumphant general, Othello does nothing in keeping. A great soldier seizes upon every paltry insinuation that his wife Desdemona is unfaithful, and "labours to be jealous" (cited by Stewart, 1949, p. 97). Othello is seen as someone who is so noble that he trusts absolutely and therefore becomes more open to deception. But why should Othello, if he trusts so much, trust Iago rather than Desdemona? Furthermore, these critics argue that Iago is an impossible character, because a man so wicked would surely not pass as invisibly as he does. Stewart cites Stoll's *Shakespeare Studies* as saying that Shakespeare seeks "emotional effect, with which psychology or even simple narrative coherence often considerably interferes" (*ibid.*, p. 83). Although Othello is seen as a great play, it can only be so, say some critics, if the canons of dramatic art permit a difference between art and real life (see *ibid.*, p. 99).

Stewart describes some of different interpretations of Othello that have been made along psychological lines. For example, T. S. Eliot examines Othello's last speech

> I pray you, in your letters,
> When you shall these unlucky deeds relate,
> Speak of me as I am; nothing extenuate,
> Nor set down aught in malice. Then must you speak
> Of one that lov'd not wisely, but too well;
> Of one not easily jealous, but, being wrought,
> Perplex'd in the extreme . . . [5(ii): 343–349]

and claims that Othello is deceiving himself, thinking only about himself, and dramatizing himself against his environment. Othello is shown by Shakespeare as unable to see what he has been like—because of course he has become rather too easily jealous. That early hint that Desdemona idealized Othello for his deeds of battle is seen in the way he appears to some extent even to idealize himself here in this final speech, as well as to idealize Desdemona. He has perhaps therefore deceived himself in seeing her as more wonderful than she could possibly be. This may be why trust so swiftly turns to distrust when there is a slight provocation: "Loving not a real woman but an image of his own creating which is wholly at the mercy of his secret fears and suspicions" (Stewart, 1949, p. 104). "In his new situation as a married man, which brings problems different from those of the 'big wars', his self-pride quickly becomes stupidity—ferocious stupidity, an insane and self-deceiving passion" (*ibid.*, p. 105).

Therefore it may be, we might add, that whereas Othello in his role as general appears successful, this may only pertain as long as his military successes boost what we may well consider to be a fragile ego. (He was after all black, at a time when many of his race would have been slaves, as indeed he had himself been at one time (1(iii): 138).) Desdemona's admiration or idealization of him further boosts that underlying fragility. This suggests that his achievements to date are, in fact, built upon flimsy foundations, and that in marrying Desdemona, a younger white woman, he has attempted to bolster himself through her. When she, to his mind, proves unfaithful, his whole world collapses around him. There is no core self with which to resist the seeds of doubt. When suspicion is aroused, he cannot hold together: "When I love thee not chaos comes again" (3(iii): 91–92); and, a little later, "Farewell the tranquil mind" (3(iii): 352). His military glory now avails him nothing: "Farewell the plumed troops, and the big wars that makes ambition virtue!" (3(iii): 353–354). Neither does he know which way to turn, there even being a hint of obsessional wavering:

> I think my wife be honest, and think she is not;
> I think that thou [Iago] are just, and think thou art not. [3(iii): 387–388]

But is it as simple as that? For Stewart the problem remains: why then does Othello not see the flimsiness of the case against Desdemona? Why does he not resist Iago? He suggests an answer, of a different nature to his earlier drawing upon Freud to understand Leontes: "Iago's villainy draws its potency from Othello's own mind . . . Iago is a device of Othello's by which Othello hears an inner force that he would fain hear and fain deny" (1949, pp. 102–103). Here, psychology appears to give an explanation, with the drama showing the audience two sides of Othello's character, the trusting side, and the doubting side.

Stewart suggests that what we have here in these two characters is a symbolic representation of the split that there is in each of us, the split between passion and reason, between trust and suspicion. Or, Othello is the human soul as it strives to be, whereas Iago is that which corrodes and subverts it from within. The two characters of Othello and Iago play out the struggle in the human mind, in every human mind, a person at grips with himself, wrestling with himself.

While for most of his argument Stewart believes that Shakespeare's characters are realistic, he owns that Iago *is* unreal; and Othello *is* unreal. But put the two together and their interaction is not unreal—as Stewart puts it: "The two together make your mind, and mine" (1949, p. 110). Bloom says that Leontes is "an Othello who is his own Iago"—that seems to be much the same view, if inverted, to that which Stewart suggests. In some productions the actors who play Iago and Othello have swapped roles for alternate performances.

That Othello is unreal seems also to be something of the verdict of Harold Bloom. He calls him "a great soul hopelessly outclassed in intellect and drive by Iago" (p. 438). He also describes Othello as one who sees himself grandiosely, and as someone who does not know himself—in fact, Iago knows him better than he does himself. Bloom advances the same interpretation as T. S. Eliot; that when Othello speaks of himself as not easily jealous, he clearly does not know himself. Perhaps he is not unreal, but hollow, and Bloom also writes that Othello cannot quite fit the play, not in the way that Iago and Desdemona do. Bloom quotes another's verdict: "Instead of a self-core discoverable at the center of his being, Othello's 'I am' seems a kind of internal repertory company, a 'we are'" (1999, p. 446). What is interesting, we might add, is to contrast Othello's "Speak of me as I am" (5(ii): 345) with Iago's early description of himself: "I am not what I am" (1(i): 66).

Bloom sees Othello as one who knows about war, but about little else. He is a representation of "male vanity and fear of female sexuality" (1999, p. 448). Bloom makes much of Othello never consummating the marriage with Desdemona: even when he had opportunity to do so, he goes to nurse one of his men's wounds. He also cites one authority who suggests that Othello's conversion to Christianity augmented his tendency to sexual disgust (*ibid.*, p. 463). But Bloom makes it clear that he does not, like Stewart, see Iago as a component of Othello's psyche-indeed, if anything, Othello comes to represent Iago more than Iago being a component of Othello (*ibid.*, p. 463).

Bloom devotes many more pages to Iago, as the really brilliant central character of the play; but my purpose here is to stay with Othello and the theme of jealousy. There are yet further ways of understanding, beyond Stewart's interpretation of Othello and Iago as symbolizing two parts of the same person, or Bloom's concentration instead upon Iago's creative if evil genius. For example, as referred to already above, there is the so-called "Othello syndrome".

In a paper of that title (1968), West (a psychoanalyst) refers to Othello as being based upon an Italian tale written by Cinthio around 1565. The jealousy motif, as well as the racial contrast between husband and wife, are major components of the original work. But in that story it is Iago who murders Desdemona. West himself notes that scholars have commented on a remarkable inconsistency in Othello's personality, with the unlikelihood that such a strong and noble man as Othello should fall so completely a prey to jealousy that he becomes aroused to the point of madness and finally to murder. West's thesis is that this flaw is, in fact, a profound and penetrating insight into an important psychody-namic component of pathological jealousy.

Shakespeare's Othello is very different from the nameless and rather unsympathetic Moor of Cinthio's melodrama. West cites two critics:

> In the early scenes Shakespeare is careful to show us that Othello is a man of high integrity, of commanding presence and simple eloquence, and, most important, of complete self-mastery . . . How comes it, then, that a man of Othello's confirmed steadiness can be so rankly abused and can so completely lose his true self? [1968, p. 104]

These critics admit that "the action, regarded in the light of reason, is full of improbability" and that Othello's behaviour is "contrary to reason and common sense". It is not sufficient to excuse Othello on the grounds that his strengths were in the military field, not in matters of love.

To understand Othello's character, West says, we must look deeper. West's thinking about the play was triggered when he encountered a real-life, twentieth-century Othello in the person of a black military officer who became insanely jealous of his white wife, groundlessly suspecting her of adultery with a white friend, and finally threatening to kill them both. Since then, West learned a great deal about sexual transactions involving partners of different races, in particular six further examples of black men whose unfounded reactions of pathological jealousy toward their white wives or mistresses were just like that of Othello. These cases were particularly interesting in the light of the white culture's mythology about the sexuality of black men.

The term "Othello Syndrome" was first introduced in 1955 to describe a series of schizophrenic, paranoid, and epileptic patients, in whom delusions of infidelity were prominent psychopathologi-cal features of a psychotic reaction (Todd & Dewhurst, 1955). West, however, believes that the term can be applied to severe patholog-ical jealousy reactions in previously well-balanced individuals of any race. He suggests that it is worth considering that Othello was a member of a despised racial minority group, and that in marrying Desdemona he faced many problems similar to those of many inter-racial marriages today. Othello may have accepted unconsciously the cultural devaluation of himself, creating an unusually powerful negative identity. His unconscious identification with the cultural aggressor, repressed and projected into Cassio, was the basis for the unconscious wish that Cassio would indeed seduce Desdemona, a wish to which Iago provides some (slight) proof. Desdemona had proved to Othello (at least unconsciously) her own corruption and baseness by loving and marrying him—the loathsome person he secretly felt himself to be—so the scantiest circumstantial evidence could then convince him that she was a whore. Finally, Othello's destructive reaction to the idea of Desdemona's deception might, in more traditional psychoanalytic interpretations, be formulated as pathological jealousy stemming from repressed homosexual feelings, as has already been suggested was the case with Leontes.

West proposes that Othello identifies with Cassio, as the outsider of the same sex, and projects into Cassio an important part of his secret self. Why did Othello choose Cassio for his lieutenant (over his old ensign, Iago) in the first place? West suggests that Cassio embodied many qualities of the white Italian world that Othello admired greatly but deemed lacking in himself. So, when Iago hints at it, why shouldn't Desdemona prefer such a man? Besides, Othello is considerably older than the white pair, and suggests that "the young affects" in him are "defunct" (1(iii): 263–264). Virile as white people may imagine him to be, he sees himself as a tired, ageing, relatively impotent professional soldier of an inferior race. Like the Venetians, he colours the worst parts of himself black.

There are, then, a number of possible explanations of how jealousy is born, and how it feeds upon the smallest signs. There are few articles in psychoanalytic literature on pathological jealousy, but those there are make it clear how much such jealousy manifests itself in looking for the smallest signs of infidelity. West maintains, of course, that this pathological jealousy is not just to be found in black men. Neither is Iago immune from pathological jealousy, too—for example, thinking that Othello may have seduced his wife

Emilia (2(i): 289–290). Others argue, indeed, that Iago suffers from repressed homosexuality and that he, too, is pathologically jealous of Desdemona, since Iago loves Othello:

> Iago's various projections may be summarized: the Moor has lain with Emilia; therefore Cassio has lain with Emilia; Emilia equals Desdemona; therefore Cassio has lain with Desdemona. All of these serve the function of warding off anxiety and enable Iago to deny by projection his homosexual drive to lie with the Moor. [Wangh, 1950, p. 208]

And there is yet another question well worth framing: is jealousy of this sort to be found in women to the same extent? The few articles on jealousy there are in psychoanalytic literature tend to give examples of men, not women. Envy (including the controversial concept of penis envy) is, of course, another matter.

If we take Leontes and Othello as examples about whom the question can be framed, "Does Shakespeare write about real people?", there appear to be a considerable number of explanations in modern criticism, whether from a literary or from a psychological point of view, that support the accuracy of his characterization. At the same time, Stewart's preferred argument about Othello and Iago, that they are twin halves of one person, suggests a symbolic rather than a realistic interpretation. The symbolic is another approach seen in psychoanalytic literary criticism, as Freud's associations to both *The Merchant of Venice* and *King Lear* illustrate, and which the next chapter explains.

CHAPTER THREE

Death and the maiden

*T*he *Merchant of Venice* is listed from the First Folio onwards as a comedy, although there is scarcely much to laugh at in it, except perhaps in the portrayal of the first two men to woo Portia's hand: under Jonathan Miller's direction (*The Merchant of Venice*, 1992), they do provide some welcome light relief. Bloom writes that his students find it difficult to accept that Shylock is a comic villain (1999, p. 171), and he admits that he has never seen the play staged with Shylock as comic. There is a record of the play being performed in this way in 1709, when a critic at that time wrote: "while the part of the Jew [was] perform'd by an excellent Comedian, yet I cannot but think that it was design'd Tragically by the Author" (Brown, 1959, p. xxxiv). If, as "comedy" was originally used, it is a tale with a happy ending, then perhaps the term can be applied to *The Merchant of Venice*, although it is only a happy ending for the four lovers, not for Shylock, or even perhaps for the merchant Antonio. As in Dante's *Divine Comedy*, there is much suffering before the finale.

In many of Shakespeare's other comedies there are subsidiary plots and scenes that *are* light and amusing, but apart from the casket scene there are no such devices in *The Merchant of Venice*. We might, therefore, prefer Bloom's description of Shylock as "a heroic villain" (1999, p. 186), an epithet that is well borne out in a performance such as Henry Goodman's (*The Merchant of Venice*, 2000), to which I return below.

The "merchant" of the title, as indicated above, is not Shylock, although Shylock is one of two characters who dominate the play. The other is Portia, and if there is one link between them it is that the Jew Shylock wishes to "lock up the doors" (2(v): 28) to protect his daughter Jessica against the Gentile men whom he (rightly) fears may take her away; while Portia's father, already dead before the play opens, has locked up his daughter's future (in the form of her portrait) in one of three caskets. The suitor who opens the right casket wins her hand in marriage. These two plots run for the most part separately, and these two characters, Portia and Shylock, only meet in the long trial scene in Act 4, when ultimately Portia sides with the merchant against Shylock.

The merchant Antonio has ships coming from all over the world, full of money-making goods, although, since they have not yet reached port, at present he has nothing. So, when his protégé Bassanio asks him for three thousand ducats with which to woo Portia, Antonio has to borrow the money, entering a reluctant bargain with the money-lender Shylock for the loan. Because Antonio is unwilling to pay interest (Christians do not approve of usury), he eventually agrees with Shylock that if he does not repay the loan within the agreed time, he will forfeit a pound of his flesh, from a part of his body of Shylock's choosing. The bounty expected from his ships appears to put Antonio at no risk, hence his ready agreement; and there can be little doubt at that stage of the agreement that neither did Shylock expect to have to exact his bond.

However, two events alter the whole situation: first, Antonio's ships do not come home, therefore he cannot repay the loan; second, one of Antonio's companions runs off with Shylock's daughter, as well as with a casket of ducats and jewels belonging to Shylock. So, now given the opportunity to call in the loan, Shylock seeks revenge, and asks that the bond be honoured. It is this that leads to the court action, where the Duke of Venice is required to pass judgement on Shylock's claim. Portia, disguised as a lawyer, plays a major role in deciding the action, so as to defend Antonio's interest.

For the present it is useful to concentrate upon the scenes portraying the three caskets (2(vii, ix); 3(ii)), since it is here that psychoanalytic criticism starts, with an essay of Freud's (1913f). A number of possible men do not pursue their suit when they discover the rules of the lottery, one of which is that they are never to marry if they choose wrongly. However, two men come forward to try their luck, the Prince of Morocco and the Prince of Aragon. There are three caskets, one made of gold, one of silver, and one of lead. Morocco chooses the gold casket, thinking this must stand for Portia, but on opening the casket finds only a miniature skull, and the words "All that glisters is not gold" (2(vii): 65). Aragon chooses the silver casket, which, when opened, reveals a mirror in which he sees his own "blinking idiot" self (2(ix): 54).

Finally, Antonio's friend Bassanio, armed now with the necessary three thousand ducats, comes to try his fortune. Bassanio is the man whom Portia hopes will choose correctly, and indeed he does, for her portrait is contained within the lead casket, whose "plainness moves me more than eloquence" (3(ii): 106). The only thing that spoils Portia's and Bassanio's joy is the news that is brought to them of Antonio's losses, and of Shylock's demand for his bond. For the time being thoughts of marriage are put on hold.

What is of particular interest to the analytically inclined reader is the way these scenes of the three caskets caught Freud's attention. In 1913 he wrote one of his shorter papers on 'The theme of the three caskets'. What interested him was the significance of *choosing*, as well as the significance of the *lead* casket. It was the one of least monetary value that was the one that yielded the prize. Freud relates how Shakespeare took this idea from a collection of medieval tales, although there it is a girl who makes the same choice in order to win the emperor's son. He also observes that the casket itself is a symbol of what is essential in a woman, that she, too, is a container. Freud then takes three other examples of choice: the first being the contest at the start of *King Lear* where the old and abdicating king asks each of his three daughters, Goneril, Regan, and Cordelia, to declare how much they love him, before he divides his kingdom between them. Goneril and Regan lay on the flattery, but the youngest daughter, Cordelia, refuses to play the game, and she is banished and loses her inheritance (see Chapter Four). Yet, in the end, it is Cordelia who is the one who brings a sense of redemption to Lear, who goes mad when his two older daughters reject him. The least worthy daughter at the start of the play, at least in Lear's eyes, is the one who at the end stays loyal to him. Freud appears to want to draw a parallel: the least valuable casket and the least worthy daughter are both the prize.

The second story that Freud draws upon to illustrate his theme is that of Cinderella. Again she is one of three daughters, although in this instance the other two are step-sisters. Cinderella is the one of least value, the one who has the menial tasks of looking after the house, while her step-sisters live life to the full. But when the Prince comes to find whose foot fits the glass slipper, it is again the youngest and least valued, Cinderella, who wins the contest and the Prince. The third story that Freud relates to his theme is the myth of the Judgement of Paris, the shepherd who has to choose who is the fairest of three goddesses, the winner receiving a golden apple. Paris declares the third goddess, Aphrodite, to be the most beautiful.

Freud is less interested in the beauty of any of these "third" women. He identifies what seems to him to be a more significant link between them. Cordelia loves and yet is silent; and Cinderella hides, leading Freud to equate hiddenness and silence. Bassanio declares that the plainness or the paleness of the lead moves him more than eloquence; so it is silence, Freud thinks, that is perhaps being referred to again here. He adds that although it is true that in the myth of the Judgement of Paris each of the three goddesses makes promises to him, in Offenbach's libretto telling the same story, the third goddess, Aphrodite, is silent. From this, and drawing upon some of Grimm's fairy-tales to support his argument, Freud draws the conclusion that silence equates with death; and finally he suggests how the these different sets of three, whether caskets or women, are paralleled by the Fates in Greek mythology, the third of whom represents death.

It reads as a somewhat ingenious, perhaps even ingenuous argument, because if we look at the link which appears to unite the different stories that Freud has drawn together, the most obvious parallel theme in them all has more to do with love than with death: Bassanio, in choosing the lead casket, finds his love; Paris chooses the goddess of love as the fairest, not the goddess of death. In *King Lear*, Cordelia is the one loyal daughter who loves Lear from start to finish, despite being sent into exile by him and despite her inheritance being cut off. She can, of course, of all Freud's examples, be more closely associated with death, since she dies in Lear's arms (as indeed her sisters also die). But the other tales and the other women appear to represent the opposite of death.

Here Freud uses one of those intellectual tricks to which some psychoanalytic thinking is prone, when he says that in the unconscious we must often look for the opposite as the true meaning of a symbol. Such argument constitutes a real problem in psychoanalytic theory, since when analysts want a symbol or an emotion to stand for its opposite, that suits them well; but on other occasions the symbol as it is seems to stand very well for itself! Freud and other analysts who write in this way can certainly be criticized for looking in opposite directions and seeing the same view.

Nevertheless, it often pays to let Freud pursue the line of his argument and to read on, even if in some respects and in some places his thinking defies logic (as indeed he suggests the unconscious does). He goes on in this essay to assert that that which we most want to avoid is death; hence we turn the goddess of death into the goddess of love. He observes that in many myths the great Mother-goddesses are both creators and destroyers: they are goddesses of life and of death. And although choice is a part of all these stories, there is no choice about death—it is an inevitable part of our destiny. The stories defend us against both the inevitability and the fact of death.

It is interesting that Freud does not use the lead casket in another way in support of his thesis, because it is lead with which coffins were sometimes lined. Other aspects of death pepper *The Merchant of Venice* (although Freud leaves the three caskets behind as he pursues his particular line of thought). When Shylock loses his daughter Jessica to a Christian, that, for a Jew, is the equivalent of death, especially when Jewishness is carried in the woman's line. Bassanio and his servant are each given a ring by Portia and her maid respectively, and swear that it will leave their finger at death, yet they give their rings away when Portia and her maid (in disguise as the lawyer and his clerk) each request the ring from their unwitting betrothed, as a token. Shylock is determined to exact death with his pound of flesh. Fleisher makes an interesting suggestion that the Shylock–Antonio pair both pursue death, and are only prevented from it by Portia's clever legal arguments (1999, p. 569). And if there is not death in this play, there are certainly many different kinds of loss.

The scenes depicting the choosing from the three caskets might be said to show the audience three types of man, in their respective arguments as to why they opt for gold, silver, or lead. Freud, however, concludes his essay with the suggestion that the three caskets by association lead to stories of three women, and, at the end of his sequence of thought, to the three Fates. The Fates represent three types of woman—almost three archetypes of woman, although Freud stops short of using such a Jungian term. Indeed, had Freud wished, he might have used the Judgement of Paris to illustrate three archetypes of woman, since they are represented in the three goddesses: Hera, the goddess of motherhood; Athena, the goddess of wisdom; and Aphrodite, the goddess of love (or sexuality); they might even be said represent the three most obvious ways in which a man might relate to a woman. A similar tripartite representation may also be seen in the idea of woman as "Mother, Madonna, Whore" (the title of a book by Welldon, 1988).

It is the three Fates whom Freud prefers, as representing "the three inevitable relations that a man has with a woman: the woman who bears him, the woman who is his mate and the woman who destroys him"; put another way, the Fates represent "the three forms taken by the figure of the mother in the course of a man's life—the mother herself, the beloved one who is chosen after her pattern, and lastly the Mother earth who receives him once more" (1913f, p. 301).

The three caskets in which Portia's future has been locked by her dead father thus prove to be rich in associations for Freud. The essay is typical of Freud's brief excursions into literature, where it is fair to say of him that he is speculative, chewing over a problem that interests him—for example, in this instance, why the *lead* casket? He draws upon his classical knowledge, and he ranges far and wide, perhaps too far away from the original scene for some. Yet his idea about the almost ubiquitous denial of death prefigures his intense interest just a few years later in the death drive, and in his view its link to the problem of aggression.

Aggression, especially in the form of revenge, is a major issue, too, in Shylock's response to the aggression that is directed towards him. His wish for his pound of flesh flows directly from the callous way in which his daughter and his ducats and jewels are stolen from him. Bloom comments that "the merchant and the Jew perform a murderous dance of masochist and sadist, murderee and murderer, and the question of which is the merchant and which the Jew is resolved only by the unbelievable conversion" (Bloom, 1999, p. 185). It might even be argued that the play itself is aggressive towards Shylock, since many critics have concentrated upon what they call the anti-Semitism of the play. Harold Bloom is quite clear that the play is profoundly anti-Semitic. There are, therefore, inherent difficulties in thinking sympathetically about Shylock, particularly when he is portrayed as a Fagin figure, a money-grabber, or as an anal-retentive personality, as some of the analytic commentaries upon him do. It takes a particular portrayal of him to move away from the stereotypical picture of the Jew, one that has historically been very strong in Europe, and one that makes discussion of Jewishness still a sensitive subject today. It is also difficult now to see the play without having in mind the Holocaust, although it should not be forgotten that anti-Semitism was part of western culture long before Nazi Germany—as Freud's own memories of a Christian insulting his father attest (1900a, p. 197).

There is, of course, no need to look down on Shylock, since he is the most powerful character in the play, standing head and shoulders above the Christians who taunt him. Bloom compares Shylock with Hamlet, who, if the strongest representation of a "real" person, is none the less "entrapped in a play surrounded by speaking shadows"; while Shylock is "a representation of reality far distaining every other character in the play" (1999, p. 182). Bloom's verdict is that

> Shylock is one of those Shakespearean figures who seem to break clean away from their play's confines. There is an extraordinary energy in Shylock's prose and poetry, and force both cognitive and passional, which palpably is in excess of the play's comic requirement. [*ibid.*, p. 171]

He may only have 360 lines, yet he appears to be central to the action, as the long trial scene underlines (4(i)). In fact, the only weakness in the character that Bloom identifies is that Shylock in the end submits to the punishment that he must convert to Christianity. It is impossible, he thinks, to imagine how Shylock can ever have allowed himself to be put in such a position: Bloom wonders whether the reason Shakespeare added this—and it is Shakespeare's addition, not in the original sources upon which he drew—was because Shylock had become too large for the play, and this in some way reduced him, in a way that martyrdom would not have done. He rejects such an explanation, however, in favour of the need to round the play off without "a Jewish shadow hovering" over the final act (1999, p. 176).

Yet this "Jewish shadow" hovers over the viewer long after the curtain comes down on the last act. It is in performance that the strength, the agony, the anger, and the pathos of Shylock is fully appreciated, as he stands virtually alone in the Duke's court, with his tormentors baying at him like a pack of wolves. The audience's sympathy for him is evoked, and the whole question of revenge becomes problematic. Such a performance cannot be replicated on the page, and there can be no substitute for seeing someone like Henry Goodman, in his portrayal of Shylock in the Trevor Nunn production (2000). Nevertheless, it is possible to taste just a little of the power of Shylock's feelings in the "Am I a Jew" speech. This occurs at that point when news has reached Venice that Antonio's ships have foundered, and that he will have no money with which to repay Shylock's loan. Antonio's companion asks Shylock what good there will be in taking a pound of Antonio's flesh. Shylock replies:

> If it will feed nothing else, it will feed my revenge. He hath disgrac'd me and hind'red me half a million; laugh'd at my losses, thwarted my bargains, cooled my friends, heated mine enemies. And what's his reason? I am a Jew. Hath not a Jew eyes? Hath not a Jew hands, organs, dimensions, senses, affections, passions, fed with the same food, hurt with the same weapons, subject to the same diseases, healed by the same means, warmed and cooled by the same winter and summer, as a Christian is? If you prick us, do we not bleed? If you tickle us, do we not laugh? If you poison us, do we not die? And if you wrong us, shall we not revenge? If we are like you in the rest, we will resemble you in that. [3(i): 45–56]

What we see here is Shylock not just claiming the right to be thought a person, as much as any other person who laughs or cries;

but also the right for revenge, as much as any Christian would take revenge if crossed by a Jew. It is possible to be more in sympathy with the position with the one whose faith permits, or even urges, an eye for an eye and a tooth for a tooth, than with those who claim to live by a faith that says, "Turn the other cheek" and yet still seek revenge.

We might also contrast here the two characters Hamlet and Shylock. Hamlet's struggle with revenge is of cardinal importance to psychoanalytic commentators, and perhaps his ambivalence about avenging his father's supposed murder portrays the problem of revenge more fully than Shylock's determination to exact his pound of flesh. Yet Shylock's wish for revenge is convincing, and the more he is oppressed by the Christians present at the trial, the more he has our sympathy. Moloney and Rockelein, writing about Hamlet, suggest that revenge has the psychological intent of preventing a crime in retrospect (1949, p. 94). If Hamlet had avenged his father, he would in some sense have acted as if he had been at the murder scene and saved his father. On this interpretation of revenge, Shylock's psychological intent is to restore his daughter to himself. That is, psychologically, a more understandable motive than an eye for an eye.

Shylock expresses something that all human beings have to struggle with. Indeed, in an article in an early edition of the *International Journal of Psychoanalysis*, Coriat states that "when Shylock's character traits are examined according to psychoanalytic conceptions, it will be found that they are not specifically Jewish, but universal, and that the same traits may exist in all men and women" (1921, p. 355). Coriat's argument is that Shylock's love for money and his hatred and revenge spring from the same unconscious sources, and that anal–erotic tendencies are the same in everyone; but as a result of racial repression these characteristics become much stronger, so that a person in these circumstances would react like Shylock does.

Such an assessment is typical of the psychoanalytic notion that almost inevitably links money to anal characteristics. Nevertheless, this argument is extended by Coriat, who cites the critic Heine: that although Shylock loves money, he loves his daughter Jessica even more; and this supports the view expressed above, that it is the loss of his daughter that is the underlying reason such a strong wish for revenge. Coriat writes, "Shakespeare with a remarkable insight emphasizes the tenderness for his daughter Jessica, as a sort of unconscious identity of the two most valuable possessions of his life—his daughter and his ducats" (*ibid.*, p. 356). Again, this accords with other psychoanalytic opinion. As Ernest Jones points out, "One of the most impressive traits in the whole gamut of the anal character is the extraordinary and quite exquisite tenderness that some members of the type are capable of, especially with children" (1918, p. 682). Shylock's attitude to inter-racial and interfaith marriage may not be in line with contemporary Western values, but it is not that long since Western society, too, had reservations about mixed marriage, and strong opinions still dominate certain cultures about it. So, when Shylock is robbed of his beloved daughter, whom he binds as fast to him as he does his money, then revenge would appear to be a natural reaction. That revenge involves having his pound of flesh, albeit from a Gentile other than the one who eloped with his daughter, but one from whom he can in law properly make this demand.

Some psychoanalytic commentators have suggested that removing the pound of flesh is equivalent to castration (Sokol, 1995, pp. 380–381)—a fitting revenge—although others have emphasized that it is the breast that Shylock wishes to cut off Antonio (Stephens, 1993), and that this appears to be more linked to the maternal aspect of his relationship to Jessica than it does to paternal revenge.

Coriat's article mainly looks at these anal characteristics, and the way they are linked to sadism and hate. He fails to develop the idea of revenge he introduced at the start. He observes that the main features:

> in a highly developed anal–erotic individual are orderliness, parsi-
> mony, miserliness and obstinacy, to which may be added love of
> money, hate, revenge, love of children, defiant disobedience and
> procrastination. Nearly all these will be found well defined in the
> character of Shylock if the development of the play and the text are
> carefully studied. [1921, p. 356]

The suggestion here is that, in Coriat's long list of features in the anal–erotic character, it is the love of children which leads to revenge, and which explains more than anything else Shylock's persistence and determination to have his pound of flesh.

There are remarkably few articles written specifically about revenge in psychoanalytic literature, and those that include the word in their title almost always append it to their main theme. (There are more articles about Hamlet's problem with revenge, than about the dynamics of revenge itself.) My own previous incursion into the territory was more interested in revenge as one of the possible motives of the caring professional (Jacobs, 1991b). The absence of interest in revenge is surprising; and especially that it is given such light treatment in many of the psychoanalytic interpretations of Shylock. There are a number of authors who discuss the latent homosexual struggle between Shylock and Antonio (e.g., Fleisher, 1999)—why, for instance, are both so determined to go through with the exacting of the bond? There are suggestions about cannibalism, drawing attention to the many references to eating meat in the play, combined with the image of cutting off the breast (e.g., Fliess, 1956). The Kleinian school of psychoanalytic theory, that concentrates so intensely on the love–hate relationship that the baby has to the mother's breast, would surely have a field day exploring that theme further, but Klein herself, despite many references to cannibalistic impulses, does not appear to refer to the play. (Nor does revenge itself feature in the index to two books of her collected papers.)

To the suggestion that one analyst makes (Fleisher, 1999, p. 552) that *The Merchant of Venice* is a flawed play because it does not actually resolve the issue of the relationship between Shylock and Antonio, others have written contradictory replies (e.g., Bach, 1999). I find myself persuaded that there is indeed a sense in which the play is flawed, since it ends, as I have already indicated in what Bloom suggests, with us no longer able to believe in Shylock, in order that Shakespeare can return the action to Belmont, to Portia's home, and to the reconciliation of all the loving couples.

Does this failure to pursue the theme of deadly conflict, I wonder, tie in with the earlier part of this chapter, and with Freud's thoughts upon the theme of the three caskets? If Freud is right, does death hover in the background of this play, but is never allowed to come fully into it? Fleisher observes (1999, p. 554), as others have done (e.g., Mahon, 1989), that it is curious that Freud does not in his article on the three caskets pursue the theme of death further from *The Merchant of Venice*, instead concentrating upon *King Lear*. Yet the theme of death is in the former play; or at least the threat of death is there, in this struggle between Shylock and Antonio, because if Shylock has his pound of flesh, he kills Antonio; and if he kills him he will himself be executed as a murderer. Mahon suggests that Freud in 1913 was unable to pursue the idea of death further because of his own death wishes towards Jung and another former colleague, Binswanger, who had split from him. Binswanger at that time was at death's door, although he subsequently recovered (*ibid.*, pp. 328–329), making it even more difficult for Freud to acknowledge his possible death wish.

Does Shakespeare also avoid the uglier side of this play by lightening it at the last and finishing what might otherwise have been seen as a tragedy as a comedy? Perhaps Freud's suggestion in his 1913 paper, that to avoid the "immutable law of death" humankind has constructed a myth "in which the Goddess of Death was replaced by the Goddess of Love" (1913f, p. 301), was not all that far from the mark.

CHAPTER FOUR

The rei(g)ns of power

F reud's idiosyncratic interpretation of the three caskets in *The Merchant of Venice* concludes with his thoughts about Lear and Cordelia—Cordelia, the Goddess of Death. To achieve this interpretation he has to reverse the situation in the last act of *King Lear*, because it is Lear who carries Cordelia's body on to the stage, rather than Cordelia, the Death-goddess, who carries the dead hero from the battlefield (1913f, p. 301). But if the choice of death as Freud's theme was in any way prefiguring his nascent interest in the death drive, the choice of Cordelia as an example may have been influenced, as Freud's letter to Ferenczi shows, by his own "little daughter" Anna (Gay, 1988, p. 433). Although later in life Anna Freud became an Antigone to Freud as the ailing Oedipus, Cordelia remains a fitting image, since the youngest daughter's devotion to the welfare of an aging father is an apt parallel.

Differing interpretations are endemic to all great literature, and if Freud has his views on *King Lear*, contrasting views are naturally found elsewhere. In summarizing the plot of the play, there is there- fore a temptation to emphasize some features against others, because of a particular interpretation. Is it, for example, a play about the relationship between generations (as Miller, 1993, convincingly argues—see below) and the issue of inheritance?

These themes dominate both the main plot—the relationship between Lear and his daughters—and the second plot, the relationship between Edmund, Edgar, and their father, the Duke of Gloucester. Both plots therefore involve fathers and children, and in both there is a rivalry between siblings: two of Lear's daughters appear to fawn upon him while Cordelia is silent; and in Gloucester's case, his illegitimate son Edmund plots against his younger legitimate brother Edgar. Cordelia is exiled to France and Edgar has to flee. Lear's two daughters turn against him and appear to drive him mad, while Edmund is one of those responsible for instigating the blinding his own father. Edgar and Cordelia ultimately are reconciled with their respective fathers.

The opening scene (1(i)) vividly sets all this in action. ("The first scene is unquestionably pivotal", says Ian Holm, who played Lear in a National Theatre production.) Lear has decided to give up his kingship, and divide his kingdom between his three daughters— but first he asks each of them how much they love him. The two eldest daughters, Goneril and Regan, declare their love for him, trying to outbid one another for who loves him the greatest; but the youngest, Cordelia, refuses to play that game, and says that she can say nothing. Lear reacts with rage and disinherits Cordelia, although she is fortunate that at least the King of France wishes to marry her, despite her having no dowry to offer him.

In the second plot, the second scene of the first act, Edmund, Gloucester's illegitimate son, forges a letter in which his younger brother Edgar threatens their father Gloucester, and this forces Edgar to flee and disguise himself as a madman. Bloom sees the play as not just Lear's play, but Edgar's also (1999, p. 489). Meanwhile, Lear expects to stay with the two eldest daughters, bringing with him his own armed men, only to find that he is unwelcome and denied hospitality by both of them. It can be argued that this rejection drives him into madness. Cast out with his faithful fool, he strays further into the night, open country, and madness. In his wandering he meets up with Edgar, who is feigning madness as part of his disguise.

Gloucester, too, suffers, first from anguish at having caused Edgar to be outlawed, and then at the hands of Lear's elder daughters, when he is savagely blinded and cast out also. Gloucester is found and cared for by his son Edgar (although he does not know his son's true identity), and he too meets the now completely deranged Lear. Lear is eventually taken in by Cordelia and her husband, the King of France, who have come to fight against the forces of Goneril, Regan, and Edmund. Cordelia and Lear are captured. Cordelia is hanged. Goneril, Regan, and Edmund die; and Lear, only partly restored to himself, dies with his lifeless daughter in his arms.

This over-simplified summary of the plot provides enough with which to look at some of the differences in the way the play might be understood. The action is set in pagan times, but Jonathan Miller (himself an atheist) none the less sees significant Christian themes, particularly that of having to suffer loss before finding oneself.

> All sorts of losses are presented in the play: a loss of kingdom; a voluntary divesting of authority, power and privilege; an involuntary divesting of subjects' love and love of children; ultimately an involuntary divesting of sense, sensibility and sanity. [1993, p. 19]

Lear and Edgar in particular have to lose everything; and, having lost everything, they then achieve a different state, as if it is impossible to enter the Kingdom of Heaven without going through the experience of poverty. Miller again writes,

> I think that a central metaphor of the play is the metaphor of trying to get a camel through the eye of a needle, representing the idea that until you have lost everything there is complete impossibility of gain. [ibid., p. 18]

The most central word of the play, he thinks, is the word "nothing". When Cordelia responds to Lear's request for her to cap her sister's unctuous words of love, she replies with the word "Nothing". Lear is quick to say to her that "nothing will come of nothing", but he has to learn that "it is only in the process of losing everything and gaining nothing that you actually are in a state to achieve everything" (ibid.). Nevertheless, there is very little redemption in the play. As Ian Holm, who played Lear in the Royal National Theatre production (King Lear, 2006), says in an interview, "There is no redemption. By the time he and Cordelia get together it's too late."(Holm, n.d.).

Harold Bloom, by contrast, does not see *King Lear* as a play that should be "Christianized"; indeed, the parallel he draws is more with Solomon in the Old Testament, and the division of his kingdom after his death. Bloom writes, "You have to be a very determined Christianizer of literature to take any comfort from this most tragic of all tragedies. The play is a storm, with no subsequent clearing" (1999, p. 493). For Miller it is a play about "nullity", but for Bloom it is a play about love. Bloom sees Lear as someone who not only makes great demands for love of his daughters, but also "demands *our* love" (*ibid.*, p. 506, my emphasis). He sees Lear as "beyond us in grandeur and in essential authority . . . an emblem of fatherhood itself" (*ibid.*, p. 493). Miller, however, has much less sympathy for Lear, and so, by and large, do psychoanalytic commentators, although they may perhaps show some empathy in trying to understand his madness.

But if Bloom places so much store by our love for Lear, he does not see that love as redemptive. "Love redeems nothing", he writes, as well as observing that "all the deaths are meaningless" (*ibid.*, p. 486). Miller, however, writing about Edgar and his father Gloucester, observes how Edgar could easily have exulted in his father's misfortune, blinded and wandering lost in the storm, but the fact that he does not means that his act in taking his father by the hand is "a transcendental one, and a prescription for a Christian type of love and forgiveness" (1993, p. 28).

Differences in interpretation come not just from reading the text, but, as in any theatrical production, from seeing the play on stage or film. Harold Bloom writes as a critic and obviously as a theatregoer. Jonathan Miller writes as a director, who has staged the play on at least two occasions, many years apart. What is interesting is to note how his own interpretation has changed over the years, as a result of his own difference in age.

Concentrating on one aspect, a crucial one, of course, we can consider some of the differences in understanding the individual characters, in addition to differences of interpretation of the whole play. Bloom, for example, sees Lear's madness as occurring later in the play, when, having settled half his kingdom on each of his elder daughters, he is then rejected by them, ostensibly for letting his men run riot in Goneril's home. He criticizes Freud's view both of Lear's madness as coming from repressed incestuous love for Cordelia, and of Cordelia's silence at the play's opening as issuing from her continued desire for her father (1999, p. 492—I am unable to trace where Freud wrote this, and Bloom, irritatingly, usually fails to identify these references). Bloom sees Freud's interpretation as a misreading, influenced by the close relationship between Freud himself and his daughter Anna, already alluded to above. But if psychoanalysts have the unfortunate habit of declaring that black can mean white as well as mean black, as criticized in Chapter Three, it is also noticeable how critics of Freud often use quasi-Freudian interpretations in order to rebut Freudian theory! Bloom, although disagreeing with Freud here, none the less himself writes of "Lear's excessive love for Cordelia" (*ibid.*, p. 484), which appears close to Freud's concept of repressed incestuous love. There is more on Freud and Anna, Lear and Cordelia, below.

Jonathan Miller's reading is a convincing one. In directing the play in his fifties, he tells how he approached it differently from when he directed the play in his thirties (1993, p. 25). Miller's argument is that Lear is going mad from the very beginning of the play. There are two signs of this: first, in relinquishing his crown and dividing his kingdom; second, in asking for a declaration of love from his daughters. Miller observes that if we set this play against its historical background and the doctrine of the divine right of kings, in the sixteenth and seventeenth centuries monarchs just did not abdicate. The same is true even today of popes. He points out that, in the present day, it appears unthinkable to Queen Elizabeth II that she should choose to abdicate in favour of her son, because it is not the sort of thing that kings and queens do. Having been appointed to that office by God, the monarch stays in that office whatever his or her physical and mental state. George III may have periodically gone mad, but he did not abdicate. When Edward VIII abdicated that was in itself a cause for scandal, let alone his wish to marry a divorced woman. So, to want to abdicate the throne and divide the kingdom is a first sign of madness. Miller thinks that when Lear says that he will "unburden'd crawl towards death" (1(i): 40) his aim is tantamount to blasphemy. The power of the role is undiminished, even if the faculties of the person himself are.

Lear then compounds this by offering to divide his kingdom as long as he gets an avowal of love from his daughters. Miller writes,

> Just as it is not within the gift of a monarch to renounce his office, so it is not within the gift of any mortal to ask other mortals how much they love him or her. Still less can avowals of love be purchased, and still less can they be obtained by offering gifts in return for which you will get a certificate from your own children of how much they love you. [1993, p. 22]

Miller suggests, therefore, that we become aware at a very early stage in the play that there is something wrong—that there is something eccentric about this king. "He must be presented as someone who is already on the edge of some sort of mental disorder, in a state of depression" (*ibid.*). In support of this, he cites lines uttered by Goneril and Regan at the end of the first scene. Regan says, "He hath ever but slenderly known himself" (1(i): 293). Goneril adds, "The best and soundest of his time hath been rash" (1(i): 294).

Miller takes his argument further, observing how in most productions Lear's daughters Goneril and Regan immediately come out with flattering speeches, and are portrayed already at that point as scheming sisters; as against Cordelia, who is silent and refuses to participate in this false flattery. But his interpretation is altogether different. Lear is an old man, and his mind is going. His daughters cannot be that young, and they may well be in their fifties, although Miller believes in portraying Cordelia as a much younger sister. What we have here, therefore, is a generational issue. The old man says he is going to abdicate and divide his kingdom, and he asks for a declaration of love. Miller suggests that to begin with Goneril and Regan should be played as shocked by this, as pausing to think, and as not sure what to say to this mad request. They do not "leap into their speeches" (1993, p. 22). Goneril starts by saying, "Sir, I love you more than word can wield the matter" (1(i): 54)—in other words she is speechless. Of course, she goes on to say something, as does Regan, and it is only Cordelia who follows through the refusal to meet the old man's demand. But Miller's suggestion is that the sisters must be played as finding flattery hard.

So Goneril and Regan do not start out as evil; nor does Lear start out as sane. It is his madness that leads him to curse Cordelia and to act irrationally. This is only the beginning of his madness. Although he gives up his kingdom, he does not give up his authority. He still wants his men around him; he behaves as if he were still the king. He says he is going to let go of office, but he makes little attempt to do so. What we see here is an example of a problem which is perhaps more prevalent with the increase in life expectancy than it was even in Shakespeare's time: of the adult child being in her or his fifties when one or both parents are much older, and when they can become more demanding.

Miller explains how it was reaching the age that he believes Goneril and Regan to be that he understood the relationships differently:

> When I first directed the play . . . many years ago, I cast young daughters and young sons, a young Edmund and a young Edgar. Now I find myself, quite inevitably, without actually consciously thinking of it, casting daughters in their fifties and sons in their fifties as well. This is partly because I have been struck by the curious discrepancy in the age of both parents and their children, which didn't strike me earlier. Why is it that this man who is meant to be more than eighty so often has children of no more than twenty? Why is there this sixty-year difference between father and children? Might it not be more reasonable to assume that both sets of children, sons on the part of Gloucester and daughters on the part of Lear, are in fact the same age as I the producer, and have actually gone through experiences comparable to the one that I have had with my parents and that people of my age have had with their parents, and perhaps also have had with their children of their own? [1993, p. 25]

Seen this way, the play takes on a different shape, says Miller. That Edmund should forge a letter from Edgar suggesting that he is unable to get his hands on his father's fortune makes sense, because children of that age, indeed like Charles, Prince of Wales, and Edward VII before him with his mother, Queen Victoria, have had to wait a very long time to inherit. Seeing this as a play that is constructed around what we now call the generation gap helps us to understand how Lear, who refuses to control his men, and still wants to be treated as if he were the king, really begins to infuriate the two daughters he plants himself upon.

These would not be the first sons or daughters (although in Western culture it is often daughters who carry the burden) to begin to feel antagonistic towards an elderly parent or an ageing and demented parent. When training counsellors, I developed an exercise looking at the various factors of different age groups. One of the most common features of people in their fifties was that they had just ceased having to parent their own children, who were leaving home, when they had to turn their attention to parenting their own parents, who were getting infirm (Jacobs, 1991a, pp. 162–174). There seemed to be no end to the demands upon them. The frustrations caused by the growing dementia in some parents, and the fact that they are no longer the parents who perhaps at one time were idealized or at least admired, leads to intense feelings. It is seen, too, in examples of abuse of older people in institutional care, when some of those responsible for their care and safety find themselves responding punitively, while at the same time the old person loses both the physical and the mental power to resist and protest. At least Lear went on protesting almost to the bitter end.

So it is not that Goneril, Regan, or Edmund are evil from the start, but that as they try to cope with Lear and clash with the old man they become more angry, and become more evil. The younger generation can react either way—tormenting the old, using the opportunity of their dependence to pay them back for all the slights they themselves caused them when they were children, "acting out of revenge that a younger generation feels towards those who were once felt to be persecutory objects" (Jacobs, 2006, p. 105), turning the tables on them. Or they may accept the fragility and even their madness of their parent, and gently tolerate, control, and protect them. As Miller writes,

> It is in the nature of human life that the atrocious creeps upon us imperceptibly, so that we cannot identify the moment when the process becomes irreversibly atrocious. Once you play these children as older, merely impatient, merely looking for what they believe is their due, you actually start to relieve yourself of the false necessity of presenting them as outrageously sadistic creatures. [1993, p. 26]

That may be so of his direction of Goneril and Regan in the first act, although Miller does not mention that it is "outrageously sadistic creatures" that Goneril, Regan, and Edmund become, as the battle of wills between them and Lear heats up. Neither does Miller's interpretation fully take account of Gloucester's behaviour being very different from Lear's incipient madness.

Although Lear is in the end restored in his relationship with Cordelia, and believes that he has wronged her, at no point, suggests Miller, does he believe he has behaved wrongly towards his daughters and towards society (*ibid.*, p. 34). He has learned nothing—he does not reach the position that either Gloucester or Edgar do. Nevertheless, in the reversal of roles, which is often a feature of ageing adult children with even older parents, we see how Edgar, in the care of Gloucester, and Cordelia, in the few moments of care she can give to Lear, become parents to these "children" rather than the children of their parents. As Edgar says of Lear: "He childed as I father'd" (3(vi): 110).

In passing, I stated above that Freud interpreted the relationship between Lear and Cordelia as one of repressed incestuous desire, but that Harold Bloom simply sees this as a misreading, and a projection by Freud of the close relationship between him and his daughter Anna on to Lear and Cordelia. When looking at theme of the 'Three caskets' in *The Merchant of Venice* (see Chapter Three), Freud suggests a different interpretation; he treats Cordelia as a symbol of one of the three Fates, the third Fate, that cuts the thread of life. It is much later in his life, in a letter to a colleague, that he makes this suggestion about incestuous desire. This possible incestuous undercurrent and the nature of Lear's narcissism merits further examination. I also referred above to the difference between Miller and Bloom in their understanding of the play. Bloom sees Lear as someone struggling with love, one who demands to be loved, whereas Miller sees Lear as showing signs of madness early on in the play. Miller also sees Goneril and Regan not as symbols of evil, but, at least at first, as genuinely surprised by Lear's demand for declaration of love, and later having to cope with the demands of an increasingly demented old man.

In a paper titled 'Lear and his daughters', Charles Hanly takes a similar position to Miller. He sees Lear similarly as a tragedy of family life, and quotes Dr Johnson, who believed that the heart of the play is Lear as father: "Lear would move our compassion but little, did we not rather consider the injured father than the degraded king", Hanly cites (1986, p. 162). Shakespeare appears to use Lear's madness to strip away the illusory aspects of royalty "in order to lay bare the human condition" (1986, p. 211). It is not, therefore, a symbolic play, but a play about the exercise of parental authority, and "the tragedy of family life" (ibid., p. 211). To that end, the first scene is essential, thinks Hanly (as of course does Holm, acting the part, see above, p. 40).

Hanly observes that Goneril and Regan are "placed in a situation of severe humiliation by their father. They are invited to compete with each other for the richest portion of their father's gift in the knowledge that they must lose to his favourite Cordelia" (ibid., p. 214). This demand for a show of love is consistent with Lear's narcissism, as is his rage with Cordelia when she refuses to give him the love that she is reserving for her future husband, whoever he may be. This, in fact, shows how Cordelia is bravely breaking the tie with her father, as children must; but for Lear this occasions rage at her refusal to comply.

Lear's rage, which leads him to make one mistake after another and to the final scene of destruction, is in direct contrast to "Cordelia's perfectly healthy, decent and honest refusal of Lear's demand that she love only him" (ibid.). She states a fundamental emotional truth in simple and direct terms in that first scene, which is at least supported by Kent's defence of her, and by the King of France taking her as his bride without a dowry:

> Haply when I shall wed,
> That lord whose hand must take away my plight shall carry
> Half my love with him, half my care and duty.
> Sure I shall never marry like my sisters,
> To love my father all. [1(i): 100–104]

As Hanly writes:

> These are the very values and truths which make life worthwhile in the face of an indifferent universe and death—values for which Lear gropes in his madness. Lear's folly is not merely that he decided to divide his kingdom and resign his authority and power to his daughters and their husbands, nor is it merely that he failed to anticipate the ingratitude of Goneril and Regan. It is rather that

he undertook all this in a way that imposed a demand for falsehood and emotional disorder on his daughters without knowing what he was doing. [1986, p. 214]

Freud's notion of repressed incestuous desire applies not just to Cordelia, but to all three daughters. To make any demand that a daughter gives *all* her love is close to being incestuous. Perhaps that is another reason for Cordelia's refusal to respond. As Muslin writes, "Cordelia's resistance to her father's challenge can, of course, be understood as her anxiety, that is, becoming her father's consort, an oedipal triumph, which she rejects" (1981, p. 153). Lear behaves like a child, and perhaps his old age is a kind of second childhood: he wants to live without responsibility, cared for by his daughters—no doubt originally hoping that this would be being cared for by Cordelia. He wants to become what Freud, in his essay on narcissism, called any baby: "His Majesty the Baby" (Freud, 1914c, p. 91).

One analyst (Donnelly, 1953) points out that it is inadequate parents who accuse their children of ingratitude. An adequate parent is able to take satisfaction in his child's independence and autonomy. Lear's narcissism does not allow him to recognize that independence and autonomy in one's children is one of the sources of consolation looking back on life from the position of old age. Hanly writes,

> Nothing is more psychologically damaging to a daughter than to submit to the demand. Goneril and Regan, whose mastery of their hostility is precarious at best, are confronted by a father whose love for them, inferior as it is to his love for Cordelia, is eroticized. [1986, p. 216]

Hanly therefore recognizes what this does to Goneril and Regan, who cannot bring themselves, like Cordelia, to stand by their independence when Lear makes his terrible demands. They are therefore compliant on the surface, but filled with hatred and fear of their father at a deeper level. This is their only defence against his incestuous demands of them—by which Hanly does not mean that Lear actually wishes to have sex with them, but that he wishes to be mothered by them as if he were now the child and they the parent.

And whereas some see Lear as coming through to some kind of redemption at the end, Hanly, like Miller, thinks that he has learned little. For example, he remains blind still to Cordelia's own needs, even at the end. She is to be his companion, his partner in prison, in what seems like a fantasy love-nest:

> LEAR: No, no, no, no! Come, let's away to prison.
> We two alone will sing like birds i' the cage;
> When thou dost ask me blessing I'll kneel down
> And ask of thee forgiveness; so we'll live,
> And pray, and sing, and tell old tales, and laugh
> At gilded butterflies, and hear poor rogues
> Talk of court news . . . [5(iii): 4–14]

As Hanly writes, "Lear is content to have her back; to have her all to himself to serve his old age, to comfort and amuse him" (1986, p. 217). Further evidence of the little change that occurs in Lear is seen by contrasting him with Gloucester. When Gloucester learns about Edmund's treachery and his own injustice towards his son Edgar, he is full of remorse, and wants to make amends. Lear shows no such realization of his stupidity or of the way he has mistreated Cordelia. Hanly writes,

> The tragedy of Lear is the tragedy of his narcissism and his violent search for a love that cannot flourish or succeed because it is contrary to nature. . . . The harsh truth . . . is that so much suffering could result in so little insight, correction or amelioration. In the end there is violence, despair and death. . . . Lear dies uncomprehending as he lived. [*ibid.*, p. 218]

This view of Lear, of course, alters the way we see him; but it also alters the way we might understand Goneril and Regan rather more sympathetically (at least at the beginning). They cease to be monsters, and become instead women who are made evil by their jealousy, by their rage, and by their struggle with the eroticization of the relationship by Lear. Lear contributes to their violence, although clearly they have to take responsibility for their later actions as well. Perhaps this is why the feminist critics, whom Harold Bloom finds so irritating, were right to argue that the play, if we are not careful, demonizes women, or, to put it another way, idealizes Lear at his daughters' expense.

Other writers also see this play as about family relationships, and therefore true to life. Paparo (1984) cites Muslin (1981) as showing that study of the text reveals a Lear who is completely absorbed by his own needs, incapable of recognizing his favourite daughter's limits, and that while he turns to Goneril and Regan, who flatter him, they have good reason for their own reactions when they show their rage. This especially understandable when Lear says in front of them that Cordelia is "our joy" (1(i): 81). Drawing upon self psychology, Paparo pursues the idea of the centrality of a needy self, showing in detail in his essay how Shakespeare describes the stages of Lear's descent into madness in a masterly way, as Lear's self fragments.

Shakespeare's portrayal of madness is, therefore, thinks Paparo, amazingly accurate, leading him to believe that the play enhances our empathic understanding of very disturbed patients in the clinical situation (1984, p. 379). This judgement finds strong echoes in many of the reactions of patients, staff, and cast, quoted by Murray Cox (1992), following the staging of the play by the Royal Shakespeare Company in Broadmoor Special Hospital. This selection of a few of the reactions to *King Lear*, from a chapter sampling the responses of the audience to that play, to *Hamlet*, and two others, illustrates how perceptively Shakespeare (and those who play his characters) portray human experience at its most intense:

> What I remember was that Cordelia couldn't bring herself to say that Lear was the most important thing in her life, and she was cast out for being truthful, for speaking her mind. I thought that in the past unfortunate things have happened to me for speaking my mind and saying what I felt. Is it not better sometimes to say what people want to hear? At the end she tried her best and she still died like the others.

> The production frightened the life out of me and it was not easy to distinguish whether or not the actors were acting or whether the action was real. King Lear was like my father, an old bigot. It was like home. All the fighting and noise.

> I found the production so powerful that I had to leave. It was like my own family—that's how they carry on. I thought I was losing my life.

Having killed and abused ourselves we are able to understand the madness and violence and the many ranges of emotions in Shakespeare's tragedies because it is close to our heart.

It was really strange for you to bring a play about madness to Broadmoor—we are so protected from it here.

I think . . . Lear needed to be loved. He was suffering from some sort of illness which led him to need a higher degree of comfort than perhaps he could have expected from the people around. He needed to be loved so much that he accepted the spoken word rather than looking into it, because it satisfied his immediate need to be loved. . . . But I think he must have started to realize pretty quickly that he had made a mistake and he wanted to redress the whole thing. But not being able to made him feel a deeper sense of hopelessness and he went deeper into it. [Cox, 1992, pp. 136–151, *passim*]

But *Lear* does not only illustrate something about the edge and then the depth of madness, nor simply about narcissism in the family. There is one further aspect worth considering, triggered by Miller's suggestion that monarchs do not abdicate in the way Lear does. Although it may not be right for monarchs to give up their throne, or popes their apostolic office, presidents, prime ministers, and prelates do resign, as those who are in other positions of authority likewise retire or some other way move on. This raises interesting issues about the ability to let go, which in Lear's case is clearly only expressed in words and not carried through in action. The graceful departure is, of course, not unknown, but there are other interesting examples, both in family and in business life, where the senior member cannot retire gracefully, and hovers like a ghost (though rather more substantial than a spirit!) over those to whom the reins of power and authority have supposedly been given. Erikson (1965), in his identification of the virtues linked to each developmental age, lists renunciation alongside wisdom as the mark of the person in mature old age. I have expressed the opinion elsewhere (Jacobs 2006, p. 149) that renunciation is also an important feature of parenting, knowing, for example, when to let a child look after himself, or knowing when to let an adolescent take a decision that may not be the right one, but nevertheless one that may teach her about the risks as well as the merits of making choices.

While the problem of the overbearing parent, whether in reality, or long after childhood in the internal world of the adult, is well known to therapists, there are also interesting examples of the effects of failure to let go in institutional life. This might, of course, be as much in the minds of those in less senior positions, who cling to their memory of a retired or promoted manager, and use that as a stick with which both to measure and even beat the manager's replacement: "X used to do it this way ... which worked much better than Y's innovatory approach". In other instances the past manager, especially when now in an even more senior position in the same institution, tries to manage his or her old department as much as the new area of responsibility. Combine both sets of dynamics and there is trouble ahead, not just for the new manager, but also for the institution itself.

In an interesting study of the management of a medium-sized metallurgical company, the French psychoanalyst Didier Anzieu shows how significant the presence of the retired boss can be in influencing the fortunes of a company. Anzieu was asked to help look at the dynamics of the company's management committee, which was not functioning at all well. It is interesting that his sub-heading for this study is "The phantasies of the father's murder: clinical observation of a group disorder" (1984, pp. 206–215). The wish to get rid of Lear (and Gloucester) rings bells here, too.

There were four members of the committee. Bernard was about forty years old, and as the new managing director had taken over from Jean-Albert, although Jean-Albert had wished his son Jean-Denis to take over his position. Bernard was a graduate of a business school, and had previously been sales director for the business. In that role he had lived in Paris, but when he was elevated to managing director he moved to a town near the factory and offices. He had been appointed managing director by the board of directors, who were mainly members of his family. But Bernard soon gave up on meetings of the management committee because the other three members could never agree. Instead, he met with the others individually and told them what he had decided. He thought that he related well to each of them and that their problem was that they could not relate to each other.

As already referred to above, it had been intended originally that Jean-Denis would take over from his father Jean-Albert when he retired. But Jean-Albert's financial errors and Jean-Denis's limited ability meant that the board thwarted the plans for his son to succeed him. However, Jean-Albert got the board to agree to a place for his son on the board and to become personnel director. Jean-Denis was thirty-two, with a law degree, and had been in banking. He was persuaded by his father to come into the firm after his older brother, whom Jean-Albert had been grooming to take over from him, refused to join the company. Jean-Denis lived with his wife and children in his father's house, which backed on to the factory, and had a door in the back garden right into the factory— which was the way Jean-Denis walked to work. But he had a tendency to lose files, forget to take care of matters for which he was responsible, and was very much an individualist. He had the reputation of being lazy and incompetent He communicated with Xavier largely in writing, despite their offices being next to each other, and he blocked many of Robert's and Xavier's plans.

Xavier was the engineering director, and production director, promoted by Jean-Albert twelve years previously when the company was expanding. Since he had taken courses on how to run meetings, on the rare occasions the management committee met, Bernard, the new managing director, let him run the meeting.

Robert was sixty, and the works manager but not a director. He had worked for the company for forty years, since shortly after it was started by Jean-Albert, who promoted him to be his right-hand man. He and Xavier had arguments every day, and both were excitable and authoritarian. But they could work out their differences and respected each other as colleagues.

Finally, "the ghost in the machine", Jean-Albert, the firm's founder and previous managing director. He was a self-made man, hard-working, demanding, authoritarian, and when he was managing director he was feared, admired, respected, and loved by the workers. But he did not keep up with the times, and after having done well for many years the company got into financial difficulties, which led to his first illness. During that time Jean-Denis managed things and did very well. Jean-Albert had, of course, retired, but continued to live as he always had in a large house next to the factory. The telephone on his desk had a direct line still to the factory, and he used it during his interview with the consultant Anzieu to check up on the answer to any technical question he was asked. He told Anzieu that he did not want to meddle in company affairs now he had retired.

It was this situation that Anzieu, called in as a consultant, found at the factory. He recognized a common theme in everyone's mind: although Jean-Albert had officially retired and Bernard had replaced him, he was still the real boss. Jean-Denis may have been seen as the problem (as Cordelia was by Lear and her sisters), but he was in fact the scapegoat for what was going on in the management committee.

For example, Bernard had accepted the post of managing director because his finances were tied up in the company, but he did not have any ambition to take it over. He felt guilty at taking Jean-Denis's place, so he gave him as much independence as he could, although Jean-Denis was used to being given directions by his father. Bernard was afraid the others would accuse him of usurping authority and would gang up against him. Neither had he ever wanted to move from Paris, and he lacked Jean-Albert's air of authority.

Looking at the others, Anzieu could see how for years Jean-Albert had tyrannized Robert and Xavier, and had even wanted to impose his son on them. They were making the son pay for what they suffered at the hands of the father. They also wanted to humiliate the father for having produced an incompetent son. In addition, Robert was bitter about having the newcomer Bernard as boss, and did not like taking orders from a Parisian. Xavier was bitter about not having been made a director, as he would have if Jean-Denis had not been given that position as recompense for not being made managing director.

As for the scapegoat, Jean-Denis, he had believed his father's promise that he would take over, and felt his father's compromise with the Board of Directors was tantamount to personal treason. That released latent hostility to his father. He did indeed see Bernard as a usurper, and Robert and Xavier as potential usurpers, ready to dispose of him if they could (as indeed they were trying through Bernard to do). But Jean-Denis was biding his time, showing how incapable the usurpers were of running a company—only his father knew how to handle things, and only the son could go on doing as he had done when his father was ill. He refused to act as personnel director, having been denied the post of managing director, so he unconsciously sabotaged the company, wanting to show that unless it had him as managing director nothing could stop its decline, although he did not realize that he was in fact contributing to it.

Each of them still thought of Jean-Albert as the real boss. He was seen as still supervising everything from his house; they all felt heirs to a boss who would not die, and they fought over what was left, each believing he should have the largest share. Bernard dared not use his power, and the other three used the power they had to show Bernard was not in charge. They all idealized but also hated Jean-Albert for his tough way with people. All four knew that running things the way he had done was out of the question. So, while Bernard is elected king, under the pretext of democratic leadership, the others installed anarchy. Jean-Denis was, in the eyes of all four, the legitimate heir, and each of them was afraid of the rule of a second Jean-Albert. So three of them banded together and made Jean-Denis's life impossible. Through this they took out their revenge on the father. Collective suicide was better than a resurrection of Jean-Albert (Anzieu, 1984, p. 212). The managers stayed late, worked on plans for reorganization of the finances and production, and discussed these matters at length, except with Jean-Denis. But there was no real communication, and unless they could be helped to see what was happening in their phantasies, the situation was, as they all really felt, hopeless.

Such was the power of the "king" who would not let go of this authority, and of the image of that "king" still in the minds of those who succeeded him. The reader will perhaps want to know the outcome: Anzieu had meetings individually with each of the men and helped to untie the knots. He got Bernard to see that he actually had to take his authority, and chair the meeting of the management committee. He should treat Jean-Denis as the ex-boss's son, and not, as he was doing, as if he were just a departmental head. Anzieu gave Robert and Xavier a short psychology lecture on how Jean-Denis had been brought up, about his disappointment, and his negative reactions, and how their attitude was only accentuating these. Xavier was deaf to these arguments, so Anzieu got him to draw up a list of his complaints, and went through them one by one with Jean-Denis. Anzieu then returned to Xavier and gave him the answers, some of which he accepted and some he rejected, but he at least began to see how the real source of his conflicts were negligible compared to the emotional issues that magnified them out of all proportion. Robert soon caught on, and he went to see Jean-Albert and chatted to him about other interests of theirs; he used the opportunity to communicate to him that if Jean-Denis went on the way he was he was likely to be fired. This helped Robert feel on a more equal footing with Jean-Albert. He also chatted to Jean-Denis in a fatherly manner himself, as an old employee would to the boss's youngest son, showing him the ropes. Anzieu also spoke with Jean-Denis, describing how others saw his behaviour as proof of his unfitness to be personnel director, let alone managing director. He was in fact sabotaging his own career.

From that point on things improved. Bernard took the chair, the management committee met again, and the change in the relationship between Robert and Jean-Denis isolated Xavier, who was forced to stop playing at boss and take up his real work. Bernard asked Anzieu to come to the meetings as an observer, but Anzieu refused—he was not going to allow Jean-Albert to be killed off, only to have himself put in his place. It was up to Bernard to play the role of managing director and resolve problems with his colleagues. In the long run Bernard's personality was not suited to the position of managing director—he was not able to maintain his authority for more than eighteen months. He eventually resigned, and we are not told who succeeded him. In Lear it is Edgar, and none of Lear's own family, who had to succeed him. Keeping things in the family, as the story of many a royal family shows, does not always work.

Lear, therefore, illustrates a number of important psychodynamic themes, both in the family and in organizations. I have already alluded to the suggestion (p. 18) that the father–daughter relationship is a recurrent theme in Shakespeare's last plays; this is going to be apparent in the next character I examine, Prospero. Prospero also illustrates, at the end of *The Tempest*, the relinquishment of his authority. But there is a different theme that merits examination, one which has some similarities to Othello and Iago representing two parts of one person. Putting fathers and daughters in one sense to one side, the next chapter looks at a different relationship: Prospero and the devil-child, Caliban.

CHAPTER FIVE

Part-objects: Prospero and Caliban

T here are a number of obvious links between *King Lear* and *The Tempest*, such as the storm scenes in *King Lear* and the storm that opens *The Tempest*, as well as that by now familiar theme, the relationship between father and daughter. There is even a hint of harshness in the relationship between Prospero and his daughter Miranda, although this is, of course, muted in comparison to Lear and Cordelia. But many of these images or themes are common ones, not only seen elsewhere in the Shakespearean canon, but in other literature as well. Some have speculated that the father–daughter relationship that runs through all the late plays might be linked to Shakespeare's own relationship to one or both of his daughters, Susanna and Judith. Because we know so little about the author, it is a brave person who would dare to assert any definite link between his life and the literature he produced. Psychoanalytic treatment of Shakespeare is often speculative, as will be seen in some of the references in this chapter. For example, in placing *King Lear* in the previous chapter and *The Tempest* following it, this might appear to reinforce the theory put forward by Ella Freeman Sharpe in 1946, when she suggests that the sequence of the several plays from *King Lear* through to *The Tempest* portrays a shift in Shakespeare's own mind from rage and despair in the tragedies through to resolution in *The Tempest*. It is, of course, an interesting theory, but it is perhaps rather too neat to detain us for long. Nevertheless, other early twentieth-century critics have interpreted *The Tempest* as about reconciliation, and as a play that transcends the painfulness of the series of tragedies that dominates the final phase of Shakespeare's writing (Sokol, 1995, p. 183).

Although the father–daughter theme of these late plays is a strong one, there is another equally important relationship in *The Tempest*, one that still involves Prospero's daughter Miranda. This is the relationship between Prospero and Caliban. *The Tempest* is a play that is perhaps more full of fantasy than any other in the Shakespearean canon, save perhaps *Midsummer Night's Dream*, where again magic and the spirits play a vital part. With so much explicit fantasy, it may be thought that there is little that is real about the characters who people the stage. And the fantasy gives room for fantastic staging, as witness two contrasting settings and characterization in Derek Jarman's punk version (1979), and Peter Greenaway's *Prospero's Books* (1991). Both films are equally flamboyant, but in totally different ways. Jarman's film is set in a tumbledown old mansion, with some of the characters dressed in torn, old clothes, and with dust and dirt everywhere. Greenaway's is set in a lush palace, with hundreds of mostly rather beautiful naked spirits, tropical fruits, pools, books, fine clothes, etc. Caliban is portrayed in a diametrically opposite way in the two films: Jarman's Caliban is ugly and threatening; Greenway's (danced by Michael Clark) moves with balletic grace, although even then his flowing liquid body has a certain snake-like quality. But if we put the fantasy element to one side, Sokol, in his essay on *The Tempest*, thinks that the play combines "a characteristic Romance plot with natural-seeming portrayals of character and interaction" (1995, p. 180).

Some critics have felt there is very little plot to the play at all, so perhaps the plot can be summarized briefly. Bloom, for example, says that it is "fundamentally plotless" (1999, p. 662). In a lengthy, somewhat overbearing account that the magus Prospero gives to his daughter at the beginning of the play, he recounts how he was expelled from his position as Duke of Milan by his brother Antonio, and placed in a boat with his baby daughter, to be cast up on the island which is the setting for the play. Prospero released the spirit Ariel from bondage to a witch, Sycorax, adopted her son Caliban as his slave, and brought his daughter up on his own; she is now fifteen and they have been on the island for twelve years. Through conjuring up a storm, Prospero causes a ship bearing his brother and the King of Naples and the king's son and other courtiers to wreck on the island. The son, Ferdinand, is separated from the rest of the group, finding his way to Prospero's cell. There Prospero sets him to the same work as Caliban does, fetching wood. Yet Prospero almost appears to have caused the wreck to bring a young man for Miranda, who, for her part, has never before seen any other human being than her father and half human Caliban. (Ariel, we note, does not count, as pure spirit.) The two young people fall in love, although it is not until towards the end of the play that Prospero relaxes his severe attitude to Ferdinand, and supports their betrothal. In the meantime Caliban falls in with two of the drunken crew, and plots to murder his master. This plot seems to threaten to repeat the overthrow of Prospero when he was Duke of Milan, and is paralleled in the play by an early attempt (that fails) on the life of the King of Naples by two of his courtiers. As the play comes to a climax, Caliban and his companions and, separately, the royal party, are subjected to a number of magical taunts and threats until the point when Prospero reveals himself, forgives those who have plotted against him, gives up his magic, and prepares to return to resume his dukedom in Milan. Prospero's servant–spirit Ariel is also freed. The way in which Prospero in the last act breaks his staff and drowns his magic book, giving up his ability to call up spirits, has been seen as paralleled by Shakespeare at that point in his life apparently giving up his writing and retiring to Stratford, although Bloom observes that Shakespeare continued to write a little more in partnership with another author.

It is the relationship between Prospero and Caliban that is particularly interesting. It would be possible, of course, to contrast Caliban and Ariel as apparent symbols of evil and good, respectively. But it is also possible to see Caliban and Ariel as symbolically representing conflicting parts of Prospero's personality. Just as Prospero changes in his attitude to Miranda, to Ferdinand, and even to his brother as the play progresses, so we see his relationship to Caliban, in particular, and to a lesser extent to Ariel, also changing, as if these relationships express outwardly what is happening more inwardly in Prospero.

Of course, there have been many different interpretations of Caliban—from representing colonial oppression of the New World of the North American Indian, to Rousseau's noble savage, to, in our own day, the African freedom fighter. Bloom recounts how Caliban has been played as a singing comedian, as half amphibian, as a snail on all fours, a gorilla, the Missing Link, a Neanderthal, and Java Man (1999, p. 663). Shakespeare's work may bear these different interpretations (although Bloom is pretty scathing about all of them); and of course his characters bear different psychological interpretations, since the characters are vehicles for projections as much as is the blank-screen analyst. Albeit, such interpretations tell us as much about the interpreter as they do about the dramatist's intention. Perhaps the beauty of Shakespeare's texts is that they are open to these different ways of performing them, since they are for the most part sketchy in anything by way of stage directions.

Taking, then, a psychological perspective, and remembering the possibility raised in the brief study of Othello in Chapter Two, where it was argued by Stewart that the combination of Othello and Iago provides a more complete person, could Caliban represent a part of Prospero's personality? Ella Freeman Sharpe, for example, calls Caliban a symbol of Prospero's infantile sexuality, and says that Prospero deals with him firmly as a father does a son:

> Dramatized literally in Caliban is the incest tabu, with more than a hint of the Prometheus legend of the binding to a rock of one who stole the fires of the gods. Caliban reveals more than the dramatization of the incest tabu. He is himself the epitome of stages in evolution. [1946, p. 29]

But Caliban is more than the rebellious son, with sexual fire, kept in place by the punitive father—which, of course, for Ella Freeman Sharpe links to the Freudian concept of the Oedipus complex. Suppose instead (for supposing is all we can do) that rather than Caliban representing a son of Prospero—and admittedly he is a type of foster child—that he represents a part of Prospero's internal world, that part which Prospero has to try to keep tamed. In simple Freudian terms, we might then say that Caliban is the "Id", if we draw upon that somewhat simplistic three-part structure of the personality that Freud put forward. The Id, or It, represents desire, drive, or instinct—it has these different connotations—battling unsuccessfully against the superego, which is represented in Prospero's harsh treatment of him. The key phrase for such an interpretation would be Prospero's phrase about Caliban: "This thing of darkness I acknowledge mine" (5(i): 275). In support of this idea, Murray Cox and Alice Theilgaard say that Caliban represents the deeper and darker parts of Prospero. Furthermore, they add that Caliban is endowed with lyric qualities—the deeper parts of our nature are not, of course, necessarily evil, and the lyrical can be as repressed as the licentious. Cox and Theilgaard comment, "Through [Caliban] Prospero allows himself to be a child of nature, enjoying the world, sleep and dream" (1994, p. 220). They suggest in support of this that the supernatural and magical elements in different Shakespearean plays, including Macbeth's witches, Hamlet's ghost, and Oberon's fairies, represent the deeper levels of the mind (*ibid.*, p. 221).

Cox and Theilgaard cite one of Caliban's speeches as an example, and it appears indeed to tie in with a more positive concept of the Id than popular imagination sometimes allows. What is repressed need not be seen as all threatening, except to the vulnerable ego. The Id, in the Freudian model, is as much about desire, which can be repressed whether its intentions are ultimately thought to be good or bad. Their example is the scene where Caliban incites the two drunken servants of the king to murder Prospero, a scene that shows him both at his most murderous and also at his most poetic, as these extracts show:

> Why, as I told thee, 'tis a custom with him
> I' th'afternoon to sleep; there thou mayst brain him,
> Having first seiz'd his books; or with a log
> Batter his skull, or paunch him with a stake,
> Or cut his wezand with thy knife. [3(ii): 83–87)

And later in the scene, when Ariel plays upon a pipe and drum and scares the two men:

> Be not afeard. The isle is full of noises,
> Sounds, and sweet airs, that give delight and hurt not.

> Sometimes a thousand twangling instruments
> Will hum about mine ears, and sometimes voices
> That, if I then had wak'd after long sleep
> Will make me sleep again; and then, in dreaming,
> The clouds methought would open and show riches
> Ready to drop upon me, that, when I wak'd,
> I cried to dream again. [3(ii): 130–138]

An idea put forward by Bloom partially supports this interpretation of Caliban: that if we put together two of his speeches, as they follow on from one another, that is, the two speeches above, what reconciles the two passages, says Bloom,

> is Caliban's childishness; he is still very young . . . Shakespeare, inventing the half-human in Caliban, astonishingly blends together the childish and the childlike. As audience, we are repelled by the childish, gruesome fantasies of battering Prospero's skull . . . Yet only a few moments on we are immensely moved by the exquisite, childlike pathos of Caliban's Dickensian dream. Far from the heroic rebel . . . Caliban is a Shakespearean representation of the family romance at its most desperate, with an authentic changeling who cannot bear his outcast condition. [1999, p. 679]

Caliban, on this interpretation, if combined with a possible psychoanalytic perspective (of which Bloom would surely not approve), becomes the repressed (or outcast) inner child within Prospero, who needs to be reconciled to the intellectually defended Prospero as much as the outcast adult Prospero needs to be reconciled to his brother.

Reading some of the comments written about Prospero, he sometimes appears to be rather too good to be true—as if, like Lear, he is "a man more sinn'd against than sinning" (*King Lear*, 3(ii): 60). That impression might also be gained from his lengthy account of his exile, which Miranda is compelled to listen to (*The Tempest*, 1(ii)). But Sokol's analysis of Prospero's character, which carries conviction, strongly suggests the need for Prospero to make his own journey. In one sense, then, we do not need Caliban to represent another side of him, since that other side is already obvious. Sokol believes that by the end of the play all the characters, except perhaps innocent Miranda, move through a process of change towards forgiveness and reconciliation with each other, and recognition of what they have done. Sokol writes, "If Prospero achieves such authenticity of being near the play's end, he has in my belief come an immense way during the bare three hours of time portrayed in *The Tempest*" (1993, p. 186).

Sokol observes first that we have to take into account why Prospero might have been expelled from his Dukedom by his brother. Did he spend too much time with his books, as an intellectual who had no taste for governing his city state? Or, indeed, did he have little time for ordinary human emotions? The latter is certainly one of the changes we see in him, and the lyrical Caliban as repressed desire or as an undeveloped part of Prospero appears to answer that question in the affirmative. Sokol observes that in the scene in which Prospero informs Miranda and us, the audience, of his past circumstances, Prospero seeks to justify himself, as a scholar, as "a superior sort of man" (*ibid.*, p. 188); and then, when he is speaking with Miranda, although he speaks of his care of her, in that scene he keeps showing harshness towards her—Sokol calls it a "hectoring tone" (*ibid.*). Prospero appears to be, in Sokol's words, "clearly obsessed with the evil in the outside world that betrayed him"; and some of his anger about this seems to get displaced on to Miranda in tones of exasperation with her (*ibid.*, p. 189). He uses phases to her such as "Obey and be attentive" (1(ii): 38), "Dost thou attend me?" (1(ii): 78), and "Thou attend'st not" (1(ii): 87), until even Miranda begins to sound as if she is protesting at the way he is speaking to her: "Your tale, sir, would cure deafness" (1(ii): 106).

If the relationship of Prospero and Caliban is one of harshness, let us observe that Prospero can also treat Ariel unsympathetically. Ariel, too, wishes to be free—he grumbles at the demands that are put upon him, even though those demands are not nearly as physically demanding as the demands put upon Caliban. Prospero's responses appear mean-spirited:

ARIEL: Is there more toil? Since thou dost give me pains,
           Let me remember thee what thou hast promis'd,
           Which is not yet perform'd me.
PROSPERO: How now, moody?
           What is't thou canst demand?

ARIEL: My liberty.
PROSPERO: Before the time be out? No more!
ARIEL: I prithee,
          Remember I have done thee worthy service,
          Told thee no lies, made thee no mistakings, serv'd
          Without or grudge or grumblings. Thou didst promise
          To bate me a full year.
PROSPERO: Dost thou forget
          From what a torment I did free thee?
ARIEL: No.
PROSPERO: Thou dost . . .
ARIEL: I do not, sir.
PROSPERO: Thou liest, malignant thing . . . [1(ii): 242–257]

This part of the scene is partly a device for sketching in Prospero's
rescue of Ariel and adoption of Caliban; but the language indicates
a tetchiness in Prospero that reflects less well upon him. Jarman
places this scene much later in the action in his film, as if Prospero
remains resentful of any challenge to his authority almost through
to the reconciliation with his brother.

Freud's description of the tripartite structure of personality,
while remaining a useful introduction to the multi-faceted nature of
human beings, has largely been replaced in contemporary psychoanalytic writing by the concept of internal objects, or part-objects. It
is this terminology that Sokol uses to describe Caliban, not as a
representation of the Id, but as a part-object. Part-objects are mental
representations of parts of others or ourselves, which we in health
we try to integrate into a whole. Ariel, too, is a part-object, so that
Ariel's desire for freedom, for example, corresponds to Prospero's
"own less evident need for release from the isle" (Sokol, 1993,
pp. 197–198). Indeed, Miranda and Ariel must both be set free of the
intimate relationship they have with Prospero. It is not difficult to
imagine how hard that would be for Prospero, who has had
Miranda as his only human companion, and to whom he has been
both mother and father during their twelve years on the island.

So, if Caliban is a part-object, which part of Prospero does
he represent? He represents that part of himself that Prospero
denies. This is partly the physical side, which is seen in the physically demanding work that he forces upon Caliban, such as gather-
ing wood and tending fires. But partly, also, Caliban may on this

reading also represent Prospero's incestuous desires for his daughter Miranda, which have to be repressed in Prospero, but which are seen in the figure of Caliban, as well as in Prospero's apparent reluctance to allow Ferdinand to woo his daughter. Jarman's film first shows Caliban eating a raw egg as Miranda tries to creep unseen past him, although Caliban spits out the egg at her as she leaves the room. A little later Caliban intrudes upon Miranda in the course of her bathing in front of a log fire, and he laughs lasciviously at her, standing as she does with her breasts naked to his view. Mixing parts of different scenes as he does, Jarman also has Prospero sitting on Miranda's bed, reassuring her about Caliban being no harm to her. Is he perhaps reassuring himself that he intends no harm to her either?

Prospero's attitude to Caliban is that he is undesirable, "filth as thou art" (1(ii): 346). Caliban angers and disgusts Prospero. But put these two aspects together and we have what Sokol describes as "this anti-erotic fury, and Prospero's scorn of all physicality, combin[ing] to silence any potential desires of his own" (1993, p. 199). By way of contrast, there is, despite their opening clash, a closeness between Prospero and Ariel, who is an essentially asexual figure. Sokol suggests that this again implies that the sexual side of Prospero is severely repressed—as indeed it might be in that situation, where, in the solitariness of their relationship and the flowering of Miranda's sexuality in adolescence, Prospero has had to struggle even harder with desires that have been kept at bay.

Prospero's desires may have been kept at bay partly by his intellectual pursuits, which in themselves may have a certain defensive quality in them. Freud observed that the epistemophilic drive, that is our desire for knowledge, is seen in the child's questions about sexual differences, and where babies come from (Freud, 1908c). Science is, then, in his opinion, a sublimation of the sexual drive, the desire to get inside, and to know (which, of course, in Biblical terms means both the sexual and the intellectual). Science, he felt, comes nearest to conquering the pleasure principle (Freud, 1911b). So Prospero's intellectual quest (*Prospero's Books*, as the Greenaway film is titled) was perhaps therefore doubly necessary, not just continuing his previous interest, but also as a pursuit that defended him against too intimate a relationship with his daughter. As Sokol observes, and relatively recent events on the Pitcairn Islands have demonstrated, "Their isolated life on a desert island may bring to mind the Biblical account of Lot and his daughters, or other legends and true stories of shipwreck and similar disasters leading to paternal incest" (1993, p. 199).

Forbidden sexuality is also suggested in Caliban and his two conspirators being harried by dogs, described in the stage directions in this way:

> A noise of hunters heard. Enter divers Spirits, in shape of dogs and hounds, hunting them about; Prospero and Ariel setting them on. (4(i): 253)

Sokol reminds us that at this point what comes to mind is the myth of Actaeon—who watched the virgin goddess Diana bathing, and for this voyeurism he was turned into a stag and torn to pieces by his own hunting dogs. Jarman's scene of Caliban watching Miranda bathing reinforces this allusion. One of those dogs was actually called "Tempest" in Ovid's account of the myth. So, in an obvious way, Caliban is hounded for his designs on Miranda as well as for his wish to murder Prospero. But the incest theme is underplayed in these last plays compared to Shakespeare's sources. This leads Sokol to comment that Shakespeare "cautiously treats incest" (1993, p. 199), and that it appears in *The Tempest* in a negative form, as repression.

Even if we play down Prospero's incestuous desires, what is surely impossible to deny is that for Prospero to let Miranda go involves at the least some ambivalence. It is not just Ariel that he is reluctant to set free. He may bring about a storm which brings a young man to her, but he also shows reluctance to allow this young man too close to her. At first he treats Ferdinand as he does Caliban—he is made to collect and cut wood. Ferdinand represents a sexual threat to his daughter as well as the means of freeing her, and it is not surprising then that he is treated the same way as Caliban, as a slave. "Both sexual contenders for Miranda are condemned to log-carrying and imprisonment" (*ibid.*, p. 200). Prospero even equates Ferdinand in his physical appearance to Caliban, when Miranda pleads with her father not "to make too rash a trial" of Ferdinand (1(ii): 467):

PROSPERO: Thou think'st there is no more such shapes as he,
            Having seen but him and Caliban. Foolish wench!
            To th' most of men this is a Caliban . . . [1(ii): 478–480]

It is, of course, possible to see Prospero as making Ferdinand prove his worth, in the same way as in certain myths and folk-tales a young man has undergo certain challenges in order to win the hand of a young woman. But many of these stories are equally expressions of the reluctance on the part of the father to let the daughter go, especially when so many of the suitors who come before the hero fail.

One of Freud's close colleagues, Hans Sachs, wrote

The theme of the play is Prospero's voluntary surrender of his daughter and, taking into account what we have gathered from the other plays, it is no longer difficult to explain as resistance against this surrender all that before seemed incomprehensible. Two of the three suitors, Caliban and Stephano, are described with the greatest contempt as filth whose mere thoughts would defile Miranda's maiden purity. The third and chosen suitor receives her in the end, but only after Prospero had relentlessly opposed him and made him clearly feel his superior power. Before Prospero will give him his daughter he has to serve him as a slave and set himself to the same work as Caliban. When the father hears the lovers' vows he exclaims: "So glad of this as they I cannot be", but collecting himself he adds: "but my rejoicing At nothing can be more".

When Alonso laments over the death of his son, Prospero says, half-jestingly, half in earnest, that he has suffered a like loss.

ALON.   You the like loss?
PROS.   As great to me, as late; and supportable
            To make the dear loss, have I means much weaker
            Than you may call to comfort you; for I
            Have lost my daughter.

The meaning of the last two lines is clear. Prospero is playing with Alonso and indicates, in words Alonso cannot understand, that his son not only lives but that he can even call him to him. He, however, had lost his daughter in such a way that, though he might call her, he could not bring her back to him again. [1923, pp. 81–82]

Unfortunately, Sachs is one of those psychoanalytic commentators who then goes on to speculate, and even to suggest that his speculation is closer than anything else to the truth, that this intense interest in father and daughter relates closely to Shakespeare's intention of returning to Stratford, and being reunited with his daughter Judith; but for how long before she married?

Staying with Prospero, although acknowledging that what is being portrayed here is not unfamiliar to other fathers in relation to their daughters (and perhaps mothers in relation to losing their sons?), Sokol points out that Prospero has the same problem that is found in all four of Shakespeare's last plays—the problem of wondering whether any man is good enough for the heroines in the plays. The plays "tend to belittle son-in-law figures, and to adore daughters" (Sokol, 1993, p. 198). Murray Cox and Alice Theilgaard comment similarly, "In *The Tempest* . . . Prospero's reversed oedipal desires are evident in his obsessive interest in the sexuality of Miranda and Ferdinand" (Cox & Theilgaard, 1994, p. 264). There is repression of their sexuality when "Prospero initially restricts Miranda's and Ferdinand's love to platonic, chessplaying sex" (*ibid.*, p. 316). Sokol further observes that Prospero bans Cupid and Venus (obvious representations of love and sexuality) from the unconsummated marriage masque.

As Sokol says, if Ferdinand and Miranda are to be allowed to fulfil themselves in their relationship, Prospero has to adjust as well. This is essential for all parents, who have to be able to let go of their offspring, to allow them to enter into other relationships. Sokol observes that this starts at the point that Prospero, in the midst of entertaining Ferdinand and Miranda, suddenly remembers Caliban:

PROSPERO: I had forgot that foul conspiracy
Of the beast Caliban and his confederates
Against my life. [4(i): 139–141]

He stops the masque, and Ferdinand comments to Miranda on the strangeness of this moment, that some passion works strongly in her father. Miranda responds by saying that she has never before seen Prospero "so distemper'd". If the psychoanalytic reading has any merit, it is as if the Caliban "part-object" in Prospero has a last desperate fling. Sokol writes, "I believe that Prospero's sudden recollection of lustful and rebellious Caliban represents the beginning of his encounter at last with his denied incestuous wishes" (1993, p. 202). The marriage masque has brought to a head the conflict between his wish for Miranda and his intention to let her go. When he dismisses the marriage masque, this certainly is a strange, off-hand way of acting, unlike his thought-out plans as they have been seen so far.

Prospero appears quickly to recover his equilibrium, immediately seeking to alleviate the alarm he has seen in Miranda and Ferdinand:

> You do look, my son, in a mov'd sort,
> As if you were dismayed; be cheerful sir. [4(i): 146–147]

And this leads straight into his speech, "Our revels now are ended ...". It is from this point onwards that Prospero begins the process of letting go of his powers and his illusions:

> Our revels now are ended. These our actors,
> As I foretold you, were all spirits, and
> Are melted into air, into thin air;
> And like the baseless fabric of this vision,
> The cloud-capped towers, the gorgeous palaces,
> The solemn temples, the great globe itself,
> Yea, all which it inherit, shall dissolve;
> And like this insubstantial pageant faded,
> Leave not a rack behind. We are such stuff
> As dreams are made on, and our little life
> Is rounded with a sleep. [4(i): 148–158]

But note the lines that follow, which Greenaway curiously omits in his film version of the play:

> Sir, I am vexed.
> Bear with my weakness. My old brain is troubled.
> Be not disturbed with my infirmity.
> If you be pleased, retire into my cell,
> And there repose. A turn or two I'll walk
> To still my beating mind. [4(i): 158–163]

In this speech, Sokol believes Prospero acknowledges weakness, age, and infirmity, and shows a new moral strength (1993, p. 203). He gains in self-knowledge.

As the play moves towards its resolution, Prospero really comes to a fuller acknowledgement of himself, which is evident in two respects: one in relation to Caliban, the other in relation to Ariel. Prospero commands that Caliban and his companions are set free, and he states in clearest terms, in one of the most telling lines in the play, "This thing of darkness I acknowledge mine" (5(i): 275–276). He has already set Miranda free, by convincingly welcoming the union of his daughter with Ferdinand; and he goes on to set Ariel free. Although we are not sure of Caliban's fate, Prospero asks the audience to set himself (Prospero) free in the last line of the play: "Let your indulgence set me free" (5 (epilogue): 20). What we do know of Caliban's fate is that he, too, acknowledges his mistake, which, if there is anything in the notion that he represents part of Prospero, indicates another aspect of the change in Prospero: "Ay, that I will", he says in response to Prospero's suggestion that he "trim handsomely" his pardon:

> and I'll be wise hereafter
> And seek for grace. What a thrice-double ass
> Was I to take this drunkard for a god,
> And worship this dull fool. [5(i): 294–297]

As Sokol says, the distance between Prospero and Caliban narrows (1993, p. 206).

Ariel, too, changes, although if he also represents a part of Prospero's psyche, Prospero does in another way, since Ariel shows how he understands human emotions. The harsh edge in Prospero's commands to Ariel ceases, as Ariel leads his master towards what might now be called a truly empathic response to the fate of others:

ARIEL: . . . Your charm so strongly works 'em
                 That if you now beheld them your affections
                 Would become tender.
PROSPERO: Dost thou think so, spirit?
ARIEL: Mine, would, sir, if I were human.
PROSPERO: And mine shall.
          Hast thou, which art but air, a touch, a feeling

Of their afflictions, and shall not myself,
One of their kind, that relish all as sharply
Passion as they, be kindlier mov'd than thou art? [5(i): 17–24]

Either a part of Prospero leads the way, or Prospero learns from his spirit, in showing concern and tenderness. Thus, within Prospero, if we take Caliban and Ariel also to represent part-objects, as well as outwardly in Prospero's tone and manner, all that makes Prospero who he is is seen changing, so that he is set free himself, drowning his intellectualism with his books, to be more in touch with humanity than he could be before.

There is one other device in Greenaway's film *Prospero's Books*, which supports much of the speculation in this chapter about Caliban (and Ariel perhaps) as a part-object, a representation of one aspect of Prospero's character. Through the first four acts all the voices of the other characters are spoken by Prospero, played by John Gielgud. Only in the reconciliation scene do the characters actually speak for themselves. Therefore, it could be thought of as an action that was taking place in Prospero's internal world, until the point when he comes face to face with those who have caused such hurt to him in the past. It is as if he is talking it all out within himself, in preparation for the reunion, when he is able to be reconciled to former enemies, having worked through all his feelings within himself.

One analyst, Holland, concludes that "Prospero is the mature man, willing to give up his daughter to her young lover" (1968, p. 124); but Sokol's more considered view might be preferred: that in this matter of Miranda, there is a real struggle for Prospero; that only in the last act, having recognized how there is more in common between Caliban and himself than he had previously allowed, does he actually show maturity. If Ariel is part of him too, he has also recognized a greater range of emotions—tenderness towards others, not just towards Miranda. Only then is Holland's description correct, that he speaks as one who has achieved the "last of the psychosocial stages, accepting the fact his life is lived, giving up to the next generation the power and the woman he has achieved" (1998, p. 124). It is not just the courtiers and clowns, spirits and half-human figures who are changed. Most significantly, Prospero is, as he had to be in order to be able to let go of so many raw feelings. The elderly and loyal courtier Gonzalo, perhaps the only character in the play who is not in one way or another troubled within himself, sums up what each has found:

> Set it down
> With gold on lasting pillars: in one voyage
> Did Claribel her husband find at Tunis;
> And Ferdinand, her brother, found a wife
> Where he himself was lost; Prospero his dukedom
> In a poor isle; *and all of us ourselves,*
> *When no man was his own.* [5(i): 207–213, my italics]

CHAPTER SIX

"Father" and son: Prince Hal and Falstaff

While psychoanalytic writing has turned its attention many times to Shakespeare's plays, the history plays do not feature very obviously in the bibliographies of books, articles, and papers on characters and themes in the plays. The exceptions are *Henry IV* and the two *Richards* (II and III), although even in these instances the references are few. Perhaps that is because the history plays at first appear more a series tracing the dynastic struggles leading up to the Tudor monarchs.

The same relative paucity of interest applies also to the plays in performance. There are from time to time performances of the histories in sequence, and at one time *Henry V* attracted patriotic attention. But one of the more popular of the history plays remains *Henry IV* Part 1, perhaps for two reasons. The first is the inclusion in the cast of characters of Sir John Falstaff—a figure almost larger than life. Yet Sir John also appears in *Henry IV* Part 2, and in half the scenes. Nevertheless, Part 2 is performed less frequently and appears to have had less success even when it was written. The other ingredient that turns Part 1's dramatic history into a historical drama is the theme that runs through it of pretence, or of role-playing, even what the latest editor of the Arden edition calls "counterfeiting". This is a reference in part to the motif of coinage that is a constant feature of the language of the play; but, even more so, counterfeiting refers to the fact that Henry IV has usurped the throne, that his son Prince Hal appears to deliberately associate with low life in order to appear all the grander when he becomes King and rises above it, as well as the pretence of Falstaff at the concluding battle of Shrewsbury.

Harold Bloom reminds us that *Henry IV* is one component of what has been called the Henriad—that series of plays that starts with *Richard II*, who is then deposed by Henry Bolingbroke; Bolingbroke becomes *Henry IV* with its two parts, and the sequence is completed by *Henry V*. Bloom prefers to see the middle two plays, which in his 1999 book he puts together as a singular *Henry IV*, as the Falstaffiad, since, by including the brief reference towards the end of *Richard II* to Prince Hal frequenting "with unrestrained loose companions" (*Richard II*, 5(iii): 7) and the off-stage death scene of Falstaff in *Henry V* (2(i)), it is Falstaff who dominates the central plays. He is larger than each play, something that both Bloom (e.g., 1999, p. 314) and Stewart (1949, p. 130) observe as something of a problem for Shakespeare, whose character seems to take over, becoming so real that the other characters really do appear to be fictions. A. C. Bradley is cited by Stewart as saying something similar, that Shakespeare "created so extraordinary a being, and fixed him so firmly on his intellectual throne, that when he sought to dethrone him he could not" (see *ibid.*, p. 129). One statistic might even illustrate this: Falstaff speaks more lines than any of the other principal characters in Part 1.

There are, therefore, two ways in which we might approach the play, reinforced when we look at where the psychoanalytic commentaries choose to place their emphasis. The first aspect is Falstaff himself, and that is indeed where this chapter begins. The second is linked, because it is the relationship of Prince Hal to Falstaff, from the close companionship referred to off-stage and which vexes his father in *Richard II*, and which is seen on stage early on in *Henry IV Part 1*; to the rejection of Falstaff at the end of *Henry IV Part 2*, and which we are led in *Henry V* (2(i): 121) to understand is the cause of Sir John's death. What particularly interests the analytic commentators in this relationship is Prince Hal's path through adolescence, as well as Falstaff as a substitute father figure.

There are, then, two rather different ways of coming at the play, with Falstaff as a clear link between them. There certainly appears to be no getting away from him! He has dominated performances of the play from its beginning, where we can imagine how popular a figure he would have been with the groundlings, but also with Queen Elizabeth, who requested Shakespeare to write more plays about Falstaff. Hence *Henry IV* Part 2, and the hint at the end of that part that even though Falstaff was rejected he would appear again in *Henry V*—although in the event it is only as an off-stage character. *The Merry Wives of Windsor* is another product of the Queen's wish, although the critics see *Merry Wives* as of a different order altogether, and do not include the Falstaff there in the same league as Sir John in *Henry IV*. It was not until the end of the nineteenth century and into the twentieth century that directors of the play began to see more in it than Falstaff, partly because the play was then performed as part of a cycle of the histories.

What is it about Falstaff that grabs the imagination in this way? A paper by Franz Alexander (1933) provides some clues to this question, but it is worth considering first what the literary critics have written about Falstaff. As a historical figure, who provides the bare bones with which Shakespeare more than amply fleshes out his character, the antecedents are strange. He was originally called Sir John Oldcastle—indeed, the character is once again styled that way in the new *Complete Oxford Shakespeare* (Wells & Taylor, 1987). But the actual Sir John Oldcastle was far from the pleasure-loving Falstaff we know. He was a Lollard martyr; and, if historically he was a friend of Prince Henry, this was not, of course, in any tavern life. After Prince Henry became Henry V, the Lollards were more intensely persecuted, so history again provides some slight precedence for the relationship between Falstaff and Prince Henry and for their separation when he became king. It was, however, a relationship of a very different kind.

Shakespeare was forced to change the original name of his character, because the Oldcastle family objected. So where does the name Falstaff come from? There was a Sir John Fastolfe, who figures as a cowardly commander in the French wars, and Falstaff in the play is more than once revealed to be cowardly. But then Fal/staff has something of a parallel in Shake/spear, so is the Bard even more in this character than through his wit?

Some early commentators have suggested that Shakespeare got his characters from a filing cabinet of traditional literary types (see Stewart, 1949, p. 121). In this explanation, Falstaff comes perhaps from the tradition of clowns, or perhaps the tradition of the Elizabethan soldier. But other critics prefer to see Shakespeare's characters as having, as it were, a soul, and that he has given them their souls from himself, from his own soul. As an eighteenth century critic Morgann (cited both by Bloom and Stewart) writes, Shakespeare "must have *felt* every varied situation" (see Stewart, 1949, p. 120, original italics). In the same period Coleridge saw Shakespeare as identifying with his characters, and placing himself in their shoes; for example, suffering as they do, or perhaps, we might add, in the character of Falstaff engaging with a part of himself that is remarkably free from constraint. Stewart describes Shakespeare as getting his characters from the interplay of their bare bones with something inside himself, and "the sum of the characters is a sort of sum—nay, gives something like the portrait— of Shakespeare" (*ibid.*, p. 121). Again, Stewart writes, "It was that [Shakespeare] took that figure and infused into it as much—and only as much—of the Falstaff-being in himself as the exigencies of his design would admit" (*ibid.*, p. 122).

Walter Bagehot, cited by Stewart (*ibid.*, p. 121) wrote, "If anybody could have any doubt about the liveliness of Shakespeare, let him consider the character of Falstaff". Stewart, always interested in psychology and psychoanalysis, refers to the researches of those who have examined multiple and split personalities (*ibid.*, pp. 121–122), and how in those who are not artistically endowed there can be a succession of perfectly real personalities; whereas he surmises that in the artist, the person who writes plays and novels (and he was of course a novelist himself as well as an academic), these personalities find their place in the act of writing. Or, as Morgann writes, whom Stewart again cites (*ibid.*, p. 122): "For what is Falstaff, what Lear, what Hamlet, or Othello, but different modifications of Shakespeare's thought?" That, perhaps, is an appropriate epigram for the analysis of the characters in these chapters, and the way in which we, the audience and the reader, can identify with what Shakespeare drew upon within himself.

Staying with the literary critics, Harold Bloom revels in Falstaff, who is perhaps his favourite character of all in Shakespeare. Bloom thinks that Falstaff's mastery of language transcends even Hamlet's, and he represents Shakespeare's wit at its limits (1999, p. 273). He has more of Shakespeare's own genius than any other character except Hamlet (*ibid.*, p. 284).

Bloom sees Falstaff as a teacher, "a disreputable sage [who] was the authentic teacher of wisdom"; one who instructs us in freedom, particularly freedom from society; he is a satirist who turns against all power. He is life-enhancing and state-destroying (*ibid.*, p. 283). He is a "great wit, but also an authentic sage, destroying illusions" (*ibid.*, p. 284). Bloom's language is replete with superlatives. He acknowledges that Falstaff does not have a perfect moral character, but asks whom in *Henry IV* one can actually approve of. Even the King himself usurped the throne, and feels the guilt of that. Prince Hal hypocritically sides with Falstaff in order to prove himself more a prince in the end. Falstaff may be a reprobate, Bloom admits, and we might not want to go highway robbing with him, but "if you crave vitalism and vitality then you turn to . . . Sir John Falstaff, the true and perfect image of life itself" (*ibid.*).

Whereas scholars frequently see Falstaff as an emblem of self-indulgence, Bloom, in another of those moments when Freudian ideas seem to force themselves upon his scepticism, believes that most playgoers and readers see Falstaff as

> the representative of imaginative freedom, of a liberty set against time, death and the state, which is a condition that we crave for ourselves. Add a fourth freedom to timelessness, the blessing of more life, and the evasion of the state, and call it freedom from censoriousness, from the superego, from guilt. [*ibid.*, p. 288]

On the other hand, he adds, "those who do not care for Falstaff are in love with time, death, the state and the censor" (*ibid.*). Reading Bloom on Falstaff, the psychoanalytic reader is not a million miles from Freud's attempts to free his patients from the harshness of their conscience. Falstaff's greatest strength, thinks Bloom, is that he is free from censoriousness: "We all of us beat up upon ourselves . . . Falstaff does not and urges us to emulate him" (*ibid.*, p. 313).

Bloom also asserts that there are only a few characters in the world's literature that can match the real presence of Falstaff. He sees certain characters in Shakespeare, namely Falstaff, Rosalind in

As You Like it, Hamlet, and Cleopatra as something apart in world literature, and that through them "Shakespeare essentially invented [that is discovered] human personality as we continue to know and value it" (*ibid.*, p. 290).

A. C. Bradley, one of those critics who is ready to see Shakespeare's characters as real, also eulogizes Sir John. Bloom quotes this "grand paragraph" at length (*ibid.*, pp. 296–297), and Stewart draws considerably upon the same essay when he summarizes and approves of Bradley's position. For example, as a taste of Bradley's essay:

> The bliss of freedom gained in humour is the essence of Falstaff. His humour is not directed only or chiefly against obvious absurdities; he is the enemy of everything that would interfere with his ease, and therefore of anything serious, and especially of everything respectable and moral. For these things impose limits and obligations, and make us the subjects of old father antic the law, and the categorical imperative, and our station and its duties, and conscience, and reputation, and other people's opinions, and all sorts of nuisances. [1909, p. 262]

Two examples among many show Falstaff to be what might be called today "a lovable rogue". Necessarily, any part needs to be acted for its full weight to be appreciated, and this is supremely true of fat Falstaff, with his earnestness and his levity interweaving in many of his appearances. Take the scene in which Prince Hal and his companion tax Falstaff with what happened on the night of a robbery that Falstaff and Hal had planned together. On that night Hal had (wisely) made himself scarce when it came to the robbery itself, one in which Falstaff and three of his henchmen set upon some travellers, robbing them of a thousand pounds. Having bundled their victims off-stage, Falstaff and his men are surprised by (unknown to them) Hal and his companion, just as they are sharing out the money. Falstaff and his men run away, leaving the booty behind.

The next day Falstaff meets up with Hal, and berates him and his companion for their cowardice in running away from the robbery—"a plague of all cowards", he repeats, apparently having forgotten that he was the coward who put up no fight when Hal surprised him and took the money. Indeed, thinking that Hal had simply left the scene much earlier, Falstaff then rails against Hal, and proceeds to tell Hal of the heroic fight which he put up against those that had robbed him: "I am scap'd by a miracle. I am eight times thrust through the doublet, four through the hose; my bucklet cut through and through; my sword hacked like a hand-saw" (*Henry IV*, Part 1: 2(iv): 159–161). From this point onwards Falstaff's tale is embellished with more and more exaggeration, as the number of men he "pepper'd" rises from two to four to seven to nine to eleven. Hal calls his bluff when Falstaff claims he was set upon by three men in green, at the same time saying it was so dark that he could not see his hand in front of his face. Hal exposes Falstaff's lies, and reveals that just he and his companion saw Falstaff and his men set upon four travellers (not the fifty of them that he claimed at one time to have fought!), and that then just the two of them set upon Falstaff's tiny band. Now, get out of that, Hal implies.

We may already have been chuckling at Falstaff's tale of bravado and derring-do, but now we can only admire the way he slips out of the trap set for him. He knew of course, that it was Hal who set upon him, but would it have been right for him to run on the true prince, the heir-apparent to the throne of England? Restoring himself at least in his own eyes, Falstaff styles himself "the lion" who "will not touch the true prince", so that what looked like cowardice was but instinct, and instinct is as great matter.

On the page Falstaff perhaps looks grandiose; he boasts his own honour when in fact he ran away. But when he twists his tale, and ducks the accusation of lying with his witty response about being unwilling to harm the heir-apparent, there is verbal and intellectual dexterity far greater than the agile swordsmanship he has previously been claiming for himself. He does not condemn himself, nor can the audience condemn him either.

The second example, in similar vein, is a far more dangerous situation for Falstaff and potentially gives cause for a more serious charge of duplicity. At the battle of Shrewsbury in the last act, Prince Hal, showing himself in a far better light than his earlier escapades with Falstaff, joins his father in quelling the rebellion of the Earl of Northumberland and his son Harry Hotspur. Falstaff leads a band of men (one imagines from behind, like Gilbert and Sullivan's Duke of Plaza-Toro!), many of whom are killed in the battle. Falstaff and Prince Hal meet a number of times on the battle-field, the first before the main action starts. Falstaff wishes it were the end of the day, with all being well for him, although the Prince leaves him with the reply, "Thou owest God a death". This sets Falstaff thinking about the duty of honour, which so often leads to death. Honour, he admits, "pricks me on", but then he pauses, because honour might as well prick him off! And can honour reset a broken leg, or take away the pain of a wound, so what is honour? The philosophical musing is like a Socratic dialogue, where Falstaff sets up a series of questions and then answers them. The result may be some kind of justification of a man afraid in the face of death, but it is also profound:

> What is honour? A word.
> What is in that word? Honour.
> What is that honour? Air. A trim reckoning!
> Who hath it? He that died o' Wednesday.
> Doth he feel it? No.
> Doth he hear it? No.
> 'Tis insensible, then? Yea, to the dead.
> But will it live with the living? No.
> Why? Detraction will not suffer it.
> Therefore I'll none of it. Honour is a mere scutcheon.
> And so ends my catechism. [5(i): 133–140]

The second time Hal and Falstaff meet sets the scene perhaps for Hal's disillusion with Falstaff. In the heat of battle Hal demands the loan of a sword from Falstaff, who is afraid to go unarmed. Instead he offers Hal a pistol, although the holster contains not a pistol but a bottle of sack. Hal is not amused, throws the bottle at Falstaff, and leaves.

The two Henrys, Hal and Hotspur, engage in single combat, in which Hotspur is wounded. He falls close to Falstaff, who has himself feigned death as a way of ducking out of his own fight with another of the rebel lords. Falstaff begins to unfreeze when he thinks he is safe, discovers the body of Hotspur, and determines to thrust his sword into him, partly to be sure he is really dead, partly to claim the "honour" of having killed him. Once more he justifies his action to himself on the grounds that if he, Falstaff, had himself feigned death, then perhaps Hotspur is feigning death too. Much is made in his speech of the word "counterfeit"; the counterfeiting of death has saved Falstaff's life, just as in those dynastic battles certain men wore counterfeits of the principals, like the king, wearing false coats of arms to confuse the enemy.

Once again, Falstaff is seen as both cowardly, wanting to save his own skin, and dishonest, wanting to boast of honour he has not earned. It is remarkable that this man none the less has this magnetic pull.

So what is it about him that makes him so popular, so larger than life; that makes us so sympathetic to him even though he is a rogue? Franz Alexander, a Hungarian analyst, emigrated to the USA in the 1930s and is best known for developing brief therapy at a time when "the pure gold" of analysis was long term work. Among his articles there is one that is the only psychoanalytic study completely devoted to Falstaff.

Alexander starts by looking at various ways we have come to understand personality. One method is the psychoanalytic couch. Another more widespread situation is when people attend a play in the theatre, or read a book. He writes.

> If we could register what people feel at different times during a theatrical performance or while reading a book, we could learn much about their most intimate characteristics. The reader of a book or the spectator of a drama cannot be made responsible for what he feels. If he feels sympathy for the treacherous husband who is caught, it is not he who is unfaithful to his wife. When he enjoys Charlie Chaplin's sticking a needle into a fat lady, not he is the naughty boy; and when he is apprehensive about the hero who becomes involved in a dangerous situation, not he is cowardly. He is not responsible for what is going on on the stage and can enjoy himself innocuously and submit to different trends of his personality without exposing himself to any criticism. Not even his own ego can criticize him, because he did not write the play and, what is even more important, nobody is able to give a full account to himself of what he enjoys in attending a play; why he laughs, why he weeps in the theatre. The underlying psychological processes are to a high degree unconscious. [1933, pp. 592–593]

What, then, asks Alexander, is the "appeal of this mass of fat, this cowardly, boasting and loquacious knight, this drunkard and gourmand, who is not even especially witty?" Alexander draws the contrast between the two heroes of the play, Prince Hal and Falstaff. He sketches the scene described above, on the battlefield, where the cowardly drunkard escapes by simulating death. When Hal finds his body and believes Falstaff is dead, he bids him a sad and heart-felt farewell; but when Hal leaves, Falstaff gets up, as if nothing has happened. "Falstaff symbolizes a portion of human nature which cannot be destroyed easily" (*ibid.*, p. 595) and no one in the audi-ence wants to see him dead. We even forgive him his deceit when he takes Hotspur's body and claims that it was he who killed him, although, before daring to touch the corpse, just to make sure, he stabs the body and swears at it. "The symbolic depth of this episode has a strong dramatic effect", writes Alexander (*ibid.*).

Alexander suggests that our sympathy for Falstaff is partly due to the contrast between the intrigues of the politicians at court, and Falstaff's relatively harmless adventures: "Why should the lords of the court be considered better than this naïve and infantile fat boy, Sir John?" (*ibid.*, p. 596)—they murder each other and justify their actions it by thin rationalizations, thinner rationalizations perhaps than Falstaff's, which are remarkably honest about the place of fear. Furthermore, even if Prince Hal changes (as is examined more below) from "a hopeless ne'er-do-well into a hero . . . Shakespeare makes us feel throughout that this change from the irresponsible and harmless enjoyment of life to the assumption of responsibilities and duties is by no means an unambiguous gain" (*ibid.*). Falstaff does not respect the policies and ethics of the lords, as in his remarks set out above about so-called "honour".

Alexander observes how "the double structure of the drama permanently forces us to look alternately at two different aspects of life which are in steady contradiction to each other" (*ibid.*). We may, with one part of us, admire the heroism of someone like Hotspur, or even the later Prince Hal, but another part of us "is only too ready to accept Falstaff's philosophy of life, with its hedonism and its disrespect for the absoluteness of social values" (*ibid.*, p. 597). Prince Hal moves from one of these philosophies of life to another as the plays proceed, and that is perhaps one of the reasons why he eventually banishes Falstaff, at the end of *Henry IV*, Part 2.

Falstaff represents, therefore, those parts of Hal's personality that are not socially acceptable. When, in Part 2, Falstaff is banished and must stay ten miles from the new king, Hal, now Henry V, does this to eliminate temptation. This, writes Alexander, "is nothing else than a dramatic presentation of what in psychoanalysis we call repression" (*ibid.*, p. 598).

Now, perhaps, it is possible to understand Falstaff's effect on an audience.

> He represents the deep infantile layers of the personality, the simple innocent wish to live and enjoy life. He has no taste for abstract values like honor or duty and no ambition. Man is only partially social. One part of his personality remains individualistic and resents the restrictions of social life. [*ibid.*]

Falstaff is the personification of what early psychoanalysis called the pleasure principle. "It is the most primitive manifestation of libido, the primary self-centered, narcissistic libido of the child which he stands for" (*ibid.*). Freud writes something similar:

> This possibility of happiness is so very sad. It is the person who relies completely upon himself. A caricature of this type is Falstaff. We can tolerate him as a caricature, but otherwise he is unbearable. This is the absolute narcissist. [cited by Sterba, 1978, p. 185]

But Freud's comment feels censorious, whereas in Alexander's article there is a sense of this being a valuable part of the self, one which has too often got lost in the repression that society imposes upon individualism.

Alexander includes the discussion of a namesake, Bernard Alexander, who tried to reconstruct Shakespeare's personal development from a study of the plays. Unlike Bloom, who would see Falstaff and Hamlet as the greatest expressions of Shakespeare's personality, Bernard Alexander sees Prince Hal as embodying Shakespeare, although he believes there is something of him in Falstaff as well. There is a delightful section where he writes:

> Who does not sometimes regard Falstaff with envy and longing? Who has nothing of Falstaff in himself? Who would not at times desire to live like him, to sun oneself, to let oneself go, to discharge one's surplus energies, cast off the chains of the world, and forget one's profession, one's worries and life-work. We wake up soon enough and find that this is so difficult to effect. And here Falstaff

comes to our assistance. There is no better mentor for this purpose. [Alexander, B., 1920, p. 197]

Franz Alexander almost applauds Falstaff's narcissism when he calls it indestructible. What makes it less disturbing than the narcissism of someone like Lear is that we recognize that Falstaff does not seriously believe in all his pretended merits. Alexander calls him "childish and sincere" (1933, p. 602), although Bloom prefers the less pejorative "childlike play which exists in another order than that of morality" (1999, pp. 297–298). Alexander gives the example of Falstaff wriggling out of the exposure of his refusal to fight when Prince Hal waylays him at the robbery, writing of it in this way:

This primitive mode of lying and the indiscriminate use of any method to save his face, this mentality of a three or four year old child in the body of the fat old man, this unperturbed confidence in his own perfection, has something extremely refreshing in it. Naturally at the same time Falstaff knows that all his false courage, virtues and perfections are fantastic, but his force lies just in the fact that fantasy can take the place of reality. The child in us applauds, the child who knows only one principle and that is to live, and does not want to recognize any external obstacle. Since the child actually cannot overcome any external interferences, it takes refuge in fantastic, megalomaniac self-deception. The combination of this childish attitude with the tacit awareness of its fantastic nature is the secret of the never-failing appeal of these figures. The naïve narcissism of the child, in an adult, is distasteful. But if insight is combined with the childish self-complacence, and indulgence in it assumes the character of play, our forgiveness is immediately secured, and our enjoyment is free from interference on the part of the higher critical strata of our ego. [1933, pp. 602–603]

Alexander also draws attention to what Freud said about humour, that what is fundamental to it is "this superior understanding and forgiving attitude towards one's self" (1933, p. 603). We might add that there is something honest about Falstaff's dishonesty, which is preferable to the dishonesty of the honest man.

Alexander concludes his article by describing the social organization of a nest of termites, where separate individuals appear to have no individuality, even if their social organization is perfect. All their functions and energies belong to the state—a community where the state does not serve the welfare of the individual, but the individual lives for the state. It is worth remembering that Alexander was writing in 1933, that he had already fled Europe and the rise of fascism and Stalinist communism. He shared the later concern of Orwell in *1984* and *Animal Farm*, or of the more contemporary Chaplin in *Great Dictator* and *Modern Times*. Alexander asks whether the termites in some way prefigure a horrible nightmare of "the future of the human race, which is seemingly drifting towards an increasingly mechanized social organization", and goes on:

> From this nightmare we are relieved by Falstaff, the apotheosis of self-sufficient careless individuality. So long as we applaud him and want to see him again and again, and expect our writers to create him anew in a thousand different guises, we are safe from the destiny of the termites. Our applause demonstrates that the portion of our personality which stands for individual sovereignty is still stronger than our collectivistic urges. It is difficult to tell whether the dynamic structure of the human personality is in the process of changing in the direction of a more collective type of man, but we may comfort ourselves by the belief that if, and when, the collective forces finally gain the upper hand in us, we will not deplore the loss of individual sovereignty because we will have ceased to understand what it means. [1933, p. 605]

What might it be, then, that makes the difference between our attraction to Falstaff and our repulsion from Caliban—since each in their own way bucks the system: each represents something of the unrepressed side of ourselves? There is something about Caliban that is more sinister and oppressive, while there is that about Falstaff which is more liberating. Is it something to do with insight into himself, the self-mockery of Falstaff as a lord of misrule that wins us over, contrasted with the almost blind devotion of Caliban to the lords of misrule, Stephano and Gonzalo, that repels us?

It is impossible to discuss the character of Falstaff, as has already been obvious, without involving his interaction with Prince Hal. Up to this point it is Falstaff upon whom this discussion has concentrated, with the Prince as his foil. Yet the character of the Prince, and the nature of his relationship to Falstaff, also merits closer examination, especially as it is one that gradually changes from witty exchanges and the mutual enjoyment of the life of the tavern and of each other, through the rebuke of, and impatience with, Falstaff attempting to jest in the heat of the battle, to the sadness at thinking Falstaff is dead, finally to what seems like cruel and heartless rejection of Sir John at the end of *Henry IV*, Part 2, when Prince Hal, as the newly crowned Henry V turns to Falstaff, who greets him from the crowd:

> I know thee not, old man. Fall to thy prayers.
> How ill white hairs becomes a fool and a jester!
> I have long dreamt of such a kind of man,
> So surfeit-swelled, so old, and so profane;
> But being awake, I do despite my dream.
> Make less thy body hence, and more thy grace.
> Leave gormandizing; know the grave doth gape
> For thee thrice wider than for other man.
> Reply not to me with a fool-born jest.
> Presume not that I am the thing I was,
> For God doth know, so shall the world perceive,
> That I have turned away my former self;
> So will I those that kept me company.
> When thou dost hear I am as I have been,
> Approach me, and thou shalt be as thou wast,
> The tutor and the feeder of my riots.
> Till then I banish thee, on pain of death,
> As I have done the rest of my misleaders,
> Not to come near our person by ten mile. [*Henry IV*, Part 2: 5(v): 48–66]

There is an interesting use of flashback by Kenneth Branagh in his film *Henry V* (1989). When Mistress Quickly tells Falstaff's men that he is dying, heartbroken, it seems, at the new king's rejection of him, the closing words of the "role play" scene from *Henry IV*, Part 1 (see below) are introduced. It is as if the dying Falstaff recalls his closeness with Hal as obvious, although when Falstaff speaks the following words, despite Hal's apparent acceptance, the rejection is prefigured:

> Banish Peto, banish Bardolph, banish Poins; but for sweet Jack Falstaff, kind Jack Falstaff, true Jack Falstaff, valiant Jack Falstaff . . . old Jack Falstaff, banish not him thy Harry's company . . . Banish plump Jack and banish all the world. [*Henry IV*, Part 1: 2(iv): 462–467]

In the flashback, Hal's response, "I do, I will" is immediately followed by the chilling words from Part 2, "I know thee not, old man". In another version of Act 2, scene iv in *Henry IV*, Part 1 (BBC, 1989), the mockery of the role-play of the King and Hal, played out first by Falstaff as the King upbraiding Hal for the company he keeps, and then Hal as the King upbraiding Falstaff playing Hal, the uproarious laughter gradually gives way in Falstaff's speech above to deadly seriousness on Hal's face, and his pronouncement "I do, I will" has an ambiguity about it which suggests he is, even then, contemplating the time when he must banish Falstaff from his presence.

"I know thee not"—how close to Peter's denial of Christ: "I know not the man". The critic A. C. Bradley is emphatic in his acknowledgement of how uncomfortable this rejection makes us feel. When this noble prince, this Henry V (who will speak of "we happy band of brothers") rejects Falstaff, we feel for Falstaff and against Henry. The question that is asked, both by the literary critics and the psychoanalytic commentators, is why Hal, when he becomes king, rejects Falstaff, and what, indeed, Hal was up to in the first place associating with such dubious company.

One answer to this question is that from the start Hal knows what he is up to—he says as much when he is left alone by his revelling companion in the first of the tavern scenes. It is a soliloquy that starts "I know you all", a phrase contrasting starkly with the "I know thee not, old man" of Part 2. Hal's thoughts speak of his duplicity from the very start in his relations with Falstaff: when he becomes king, what a contrast that will be with his reputation as a young man, that he will the more be "wonder'd at":

> I know you all, and will awhile uphold
> The unyok'd humour of your idleness;
> Yet herein will I imitate the sun,
> Who doth permit the base contagious clouds
> To smother up his beauty from the world,
> That, when he please again to be himself,
> Being wanted, he may be more wonder'd at
> By breaking through the foul and ugly mists
> Of vapours that did seem to strangle him.
> . . . So, when this loose behaviour I throw off
> And pay the debt I never promised

By how much better than my word I am,
By so much shall I falsify men's hopes;
And, like bright metal on a sullen ground,
My reformation, glitt'ring o'er my fault,
Shall show more goodly and attract more eyes
Than that which hath no foil to set it off.
I'll so offend to make offence a skill,
Redeeming time when men think least I will. [1(ii): 187–210]

Bloom notes that from the very start Hal is in fact on the attack, and even if Falstaff replies wittily, Bloom thinks that he must already recognize that the Prince is ambivalent. Hal is playing a part, from the very start, to make his conversion to hero-king all the more obvious. He is playing a role, an idea that Peter Murray concentrates upon, from a cognitive–behavioural perspective, in the chapter on Prince Hal in his book *Shakespeare's Imagined Persons*. One obvious role-playing scene is that which has already been referred to above, in Act 2, scene iv, where Falstaff plays the part of Hal's father, Henry IV, and Hal plays himself. This role-play bears out the father–son relationship that Falstaff and Hal appear to have, with the Falstaff father figure being completely different in personality from Hal's actual father, Henry IV. But, as Bloom observes, how different the "play" is when they swap roles, when Hal plays the King and Falstaff the son. I have already noted the way the mockery turns to deadly seriousness, and Bloom observes how Hal shows his "cold fury", whereas Falstaff as King is so much milder to the son (1999, p. 301). As Bloom notes, whereas Falstaff role-plays, when it comes to Hal's turn to play the king we see evidence of his true colours. In role he is not actually play-acting. He is being himself. In the apparent humour of this part of the action, there is evidence of the return of the *suppressed* side of himself, suppressed consciously for his own purposes. Falstaff comes across as transparent; but we detect the deceitfulness in Hal.

Stewart (1949, p. 138), building partly on the role-playing scene in the tavern, and partly drawing upon the same sources as Freud does in his theories in *Totem and Taboo* (1912–1913) suggests that one reason for the rejection of Falstaff is because Hal needs to kill off Falstaff, in place of killing his father the king. Perhaps, suggests Stewart, Falstaff is like the sacrificial king of Frazer's *Golden Bough*, the scapegoat who must be sacrificed at the start of the new reign.

And if, indeed, Falstaff is a father figure who must be "killed off" in the process of Prince Hal's maturing through adolescence—and adolescence is the theme picked up by several psychoanalyst commentators—then this reflects what Winnicott wrote about the relationship between adolescents and parents. Winnicott at one point discusses the game "I'm the King of the Castle"—how the dirty rascal knocks the king over and in turn becomes king. Winnicott does not himself allude to Henry Bolingbroke pushing Richard II off the throne and becoming king himself, but he goes on:

> We need to translate this childhood game into the language of the unconscious motivation of adolescence and society. If the child is to become adult, then this move is achieved over the dead body of an adult . . . In the total unconscious fantasy belonging to growth at puberty and in adolescence, there is the death of someone. A great deal can be managed in play and by displacement, and on the basis of cross-identification. In the psychotherapy of the individual adolescent . . . there is to be found death and personal triumph as something inherent in the process of maturation and in the acquisition of adult status. [1971, p. 45]

The reference to cross-identification links with the relationship between Falstaff and Prince Hal, and the role-playing scene where there is indeed obvious cross-identification.

Other psychoanalytic commentators pursue this type of interpretation of the play, although they tend to use the word "oedipal" more frequently than Winnicott does. Winnicott does not limit the adolescent–parental struggle to sons and fathers, whereas those who write about *Henry IV* do—perhaps because there are, in fact, not many women who feature strongly at court. Hal's struggle with his father is emphasized. Aarons (1970) observes how Henry IV appears to see his son's behaviour as a type of revenge for his own seizing of the crown. Perhaps he indulges his son too much, or so Aarons suggests: "Parental guilt is one motivation for indulging the adolescent. It is passive and filled with a despair" (*ibid.*, p. 331). Aarons explores the king–prince relationship as an example of the need for a strong parent to set boundaries for the adolescent, who wishes to replace the parent as "king of the castle". The play itself implies the absence of such boundaries. Aarons also draws attention to a scene towards the end of Part 2, where Prince Hal walks off with the royal crown when his sleeping father lies dying. This symbolizes the wish to replace the parent figure, although another side of the relationship is seen where Prince Hal rescues his father at the Battle of Shrewsbury and kills his attacker. In a different article, Faber (1967) produces a number of examples of the oedipal conflict, including Hotspur and his father, as well as Hotspur's rebellion against the king. Ernst Kris writes similarly, that "Hotspur's rebellion represents also Prince Hal's unconscious parricidal impulses" (1948, p. 493), although "in shunning the court for the tavern he expresses his hostility to his father and escapes the temptation to parricide" (*ibid.*, p. 498).

Cited in an article on irony (Stein, 1985), Muecke introduces the figure of the Lord Chief Justice in Part 2 as being the antithesis of Falstaff. He observes how Prince Hal is like the ego, caught between the id (Falstaff) and the superego (The Lord Chief Justice):

> We can look upon the Ego as being in an ironic predicament, caught between the amoral, irresponsible, nonconforming Id and the moral, responsible conforming Superego, much like Prince Hal between Falstaff and the Lord Chief Justice, the former life-giving and dynamic, the latter life-denying and orderly-the irony lies in the contradictory opposition of values; we feel we must be for and against both sides. [Muecke, 1969, p. 142]

Finally, and by way of summing up the Henriad, Lichtenberg and Lichtenberg (1969) cite a leading Shakespearean critic, John Dover Wilson (1944), as calling the *Henry IV* plays the story of the education of a prince. They conclude that *Henry IV* Parts 1 and 2, by their shifting scenes between council chamber and tavern and the parody of serious matters by the comic, show the adolescent Prince Hal negotiating two very different views of life:

> The ideal at which he finally arrives on assuming kingship is not the mode of his father, Henry IV, and his brand of feudal civil quarrels; nor is it the lawless epicurean ways of Falstaff and his cronies. Hal, learning through examining and experiencing first one and then the other, absorbs the "lessons" and emerges from this adolescent labyrinth with his own mature form of kingship. [Lichtenberg & Lichtenberg, 1969, p. 882]

They also refer to the role of humour as being a way of reducing some of the threats of life to something more comfortable. They quote from Freud's essay on humour (1927d), where he describes how through humour "the ego refuses to be distressed by the provocations of reality, to let itself be compelled to suffer" (Lichtenberg & Lichtenberg, 1969, p. 162). Humour, in other words, makes light of the serious, reduces it down to size, and tells us we must not be afraid of that which humour mocks. But they also quote Freud's phrase: "Humour is not resigned; it is rebellious" (*ibid.*, p. 163), showing that humour need not be seen as escapism. The Lichtenbergs suggest that this might be what the Falstaff scenes do for the audience—they put us in touch with our adolescent side, and enable us both to laugh at it, while at the same time reminding us of our early ideals before those aspirations were, to differing degrees, corrupted by the reality of adult life.

Although there are moments of humour in *The Merchant of Venice* (the first two casket scenes can be played so), there are few other plays in this book that raise a smile. King Lear has wit (although the relationship with his Fool has not been examined in that chapter). Falstaff has wit, but he also makes us laugh, and it is perhaps appropriate to conclude this chapter with this reference to humour. Freud's essay (1927d) reinforces its value, and many of Freud's phrases could be applied to Falstaff. Freud may have been censorious of Falstaff's narcissism, but in these passages Freud is much more positive about narcissism, and helps us further to understand the magnetic qualities of Falstaff's character:

> Humour has in it a *liberating* element. But it has also something fine and elevating . . . Obviously, what is fine about it is the triumph of narcissism, the ego's victorious assertion of its own invulnerability. It refuses to be hurt by the arrows of reality or to be compelled to suffer. It insists that it is impervious to wounds dealt by the outside world, in fact, that these are merely occasions for affording it pleasure. This last trait is a fundamental characteristic of humour. [1927d, p. 162, Freud's emphasis]

> Further, we note that it is not everyone who is capable of the humorous attitude: it is a rare and precious gift. [*ibid.*, pp. 166]

CHAPTER SEVEN

The Macbeths: a childless couple?

Father and daughter, father and son—these have been prominent themes in earlier chapters. Coming to *Macbeth* one of the
major issues, at least as posited in psychoanalytic writing, is
the principal characters' childlessness. Instead, it is often
commented, the parent–child relationship is played out within the
marriage of Macbeth and his wife.

This, for example, is the argument put forward by Hildebrand
in a chapter titled "The Caledonian tragedy" (2006). Hildebrand
chooses his title from one of several alternative names used in the
theatre for Macbeth, since there is a superstition amongst actors that
the actual name of Shakespeare's tragedy should never be spoken
aloud in a theatre. Better known is the title "The Scottish Play",
although there are others that Hildebrand refers to, such as "Harry
Lauder", "That Play" or "The Unmentionable". Citing material
from a book on the play by Huggett (1981), Hildebrand refers to a
history of disasters associated with the staging of the play: "theatres
collapsing, actors falling ill, being injured in stage fights, running
away, breaking down and actresses miscarrying" (Hildebrand,
2006, p. 44). Actors playing the leading roles are said to have died
soon after the play opened and many productions have been

associated with dreadful experiences for the cast. Because of the play's popularity, it was often thought that the company must be about to close when it was put on, because the management were trying to get the audience into the theatre to save the company from financial collapse. There have apparently been actual deaths in stage duels; and The Royal Shakespeare Theatre at Stratford-on-Avon burned down in the 1930s on the night following a performance of *Macbeth*.

Hildebrand further explains that if an actor does quote *Macbeth*, he or she must immediately go through a series of rituals in order to counteract the curse of the play. The traditional ritual is "To go out of the dressing room, turn round three times, to spit and knock on the door three times and beg humbly for re-admission" (Huggett, 1981, p. 62). A weaker alternative is to quote a line from *The Merchant of Venice*, which is seen as a lucky play, "Fair thoughts and happy hours attend on you".

Hildebrand's chapter begins with an attempt to explain this superstition in the theatrical profession. Initially, he quotes the theatrical director Peter Hall (1982) on one of the major themes:

> *Macbeth* is the most thorough-going study of evil that I know in dramatic literature. Evil in every sense: cosmic sickness, personal sickness, personal neurosis, the consequence of sin, the repentance of sin, blood leading to more blood, and that in a way leading inevitably to regeneration. Disease of crime or evil induces death, which induces life: *Macbeth* presents this cycle of living and in that sense I find it the most metaphysical of Shakespeare's plays—an unblinking look at the nature of evil in the person and in the state and in the cosmos. (1982, p. 16).

So, is the superstition to keep evil at bay? Hildebrand thinks otherwise, believing that it is a play about mother–son incest, and by implication that it is this idea that needs to be kept at bay. He uses the term incest broadly, but his intention is to show that Macbeth weds someone who is the age of his mother—at least that is the way he would like to see the casting of the two characters in respect of their ages, with Lady Macbeth considerably older than Macbeth. Although he has never seen such a casting himself, the Royal Shakespeare Company's 1978 production, directed by Trevor

Nunn and available on DVD, casts Ian McKellen as Macbeth and Judi Dench as Lady Macbeth, Dench looking rather older than McKellen.

It is interesting, too, that Harold Bloom, who I have already made clear is no friend of psychoanalysis, actually thinks himself that Lady Macbeth is, until she goes mad, "as much Macbeth's mother as his wife" (1999, p. 522). Bloom is actually in this instance more complimentary to Freud, thinking he is "shrewder on Macbeth" (*ibid.*) and that Freud's attempt at explaining why Lady Macbeth goes mad, as others indeed suggest, is to do with what Freud identifies as her childlessness (1916d). It is a view with which Bloom has some sympathy. Freud contrasts this childlessness with the constant references in the play to the father–child relationship (*ibid.*, p. 321). "I believe that Lady Macbeth's illness, the transformation of her callousness into penitence, could be explained directly as a reaction to her childlessness, by which she is convinced of her impotence against the decrees of nature" (*ibid.*, p. 322).

Freud's discussion of Lady Macbeth occurs in a paper on character types. In it he tries to understand both the doubt and cowardice in Macbeth, and the subsequent illness of Lady Macbeth. He suggests that the crime that the Macbeths committed (that is, regicide and then infanticide) was a violation of the laws of geniture and that the punishment was their childlessness. This is, of course, a reversal of the order of events in the play if we are to believe in the theory of their childlessness. But with Freud we are often dealing with unconscious links that have no regard for time. Nevertheless, it is not surprising that, despite this suggestion, Freud could not establish the nature of the relationship between the crime and the punishment, or find the reason that linked either the frustration or success of Lady Macbeth's plan to the symptoms of her illness.

Freud is interested in his essay as to why some people, like Lady Macbeth, "forged from the toughest metal" (1916d, p. 320), founder right at the point of fulfilment of their aims (*ibid.*, p. 318), even if in this case the aim is a murderous one; that is, through murder to place her husband on the throne of Scotland. He writes: "So much the more surprising, and indeed bewildering, must it appear when as a doctor one makes the discovery that people occasionally fall ill precisely when a deeply-rooted and long-cherished wish has come to fulfilment" (*ibid.*, p. 316). He believes at one point that the explanation lies in the power of her conscience.

Nevertheless, despite toying with these various possibilities, actually Freud remains stumped as to a convincing explanation of Lady Macbeth's madness. He owns that he is not convinced that he has understood her character, and finally leans more towards a theory put forward by a colleague: that Macbeth and Lady Macbeth represent two parts of the same person (*ibid.*, p. 324). This type of explanation of some of Shakespeare's characters has already been examined above in the chapters on Othello (and Iago) and Prospero (and Caliban). There are also hints in Freud's short essay on the Macbeths, although he does not use the term, of a kind of *folie à deux*, a particular psychiatric phenomenon to which I return below.

The plot of *Macbeth*, one of the shortest of Shakespeare's plays, is simple to recall since it only has a single thread running through it—the rise and fall of Macbeth and his wife. Macbeth, a heroic Scottish chieftain, learns from the oracular pronouncements of three witches that he is to succeed first to the title of Thane of Cawdor, and then become King of Scotland; at the same time he is told that the progeny of his companion Banquo will eventually accede to the throne. When Macbeth is made Thane of Cawdor by King Duncan, thus fulfilling the witches' prophecy, Macbeth is pushed by his ambition and the forcefulness of his wife to take the throne, murdering the king, Duncan, when he comes to stay. Macbeth thus takes the throne, although Duncan's sons flee the country. Faced with the prophecy about Banquo's line taking the throne, Macbeth orders Banquo's death, although Banquo's son also escapes. From this high point of success the fortunes of Macbeth and Lady Macbeth take a downward turn: Lady Macbeth goes mad, and Macbeth, despite trying to get rid of other contenders in line for the throne, is defeated and killed in battle by the sons of the murdered king.

As Peter Hall writes, "the dramatization of the relationship between Lady Macbeth and Macbeth *makes* the story happen. There are political ramifications, but the extraordinary basic tension is that between a great warrior, a great physical leader, and his wife" (1982, p. 17, original emphasis). Hildebrand quotes Hall at some length:

Macbeth is capable of hand-to-hand fighting and has enormous charisma, so that success comes naturally, but he is not in any sense an extrovert. His mask is that of an extrovert, but his actual sense is introverted, with a deep imagination, and a sense of fantasy with a rapid feverish ability to proceed from consequence to consequence like someone in a dream or nightmare. His imagination, even when he is happy and at peace, is restless. He is very perceptive, he studies himself . . . Macbeth knows himself, his own imagination, but Lady Macbeth has a very limited imagination, and this is why some actresses find the part unsatisfactory: they try to make it more than it is. I think it is a great role because she is a woman with little fantasy, little imagination, who is thoroughly practical, and thoroughly pragmatic. She is also very, very sexy; that is one of her holds on him, as it is one of his holds on her. [Hall, 1982, p. 17]

Hildebrand goes on:

Macbeth is a very martial man who is actually sensitive, poetic, and, in the best sense, feminine. He is always seeking these aspects of himself. Lady Macbeth is trying to complete herself to gain power through her identification with the martial hero. Each complements the other, and I think this is the source of their extra-ordinary capacity to understand and be close to one another. [2006, pp. 47–48]

That is a slightly different way of seeing the couple than Freud's idea that they represent two parts of a whole. Hildebrand's idea is much more that they complement one another, providing for each other what is weak in themselves but strong in the other.

Hildebrand's hypothesis is that Macbeth supplanted his father upon his father's death; and then that he replaced Cawdor in Lady Macbeth's bed. However, it is not at all clear on what grounds Hildebrand assumes that Cawdor stands for Lady Macbeth's first husband. He reckons that Macbeth marries Lady Macbeth "for her sexual passion, for her femininity, and to gain entrée into the royal circle" (*ibid.*, p. 49), and so gain the opportunity of becoming king. Lady Macbeth takes Macbeth "for his force, his potency, and the possibility of controlling through him the springs of power" (*ibid.*, pp. 49–50). There are, however, other analysts who comment more on Lady Macbeth's masculinity and potency, while Hildebrand has already written earlier, as quoted above, that Macbeth is "in the best sense, feminine" (*ibid.*, p. 47). This does appear to be another of those examples of having your cake and eating it!

Much of what Hildebrand writes here is speculation, although it does, of course, fit his theory that the young Macbeth married an older woman, past child-bearing age, so that their relationship is, age-wise as well as psychologically, more like mother–son than husband and wife. Against this interpretation there is, for example, Susan Bachmann's: "Macbeth's inability to assert himself is heightened by his implied impotency and sterility-never a real father, he withdraws into the role of son where he feels 'cabined, cribbed, confined, bound in to saucy doubts and fears' (3(iv))" (1978, p. 98). She observes that Lady Macbeth is the stronger of the two, and that

> while purporting to strengthen Macbeth's manhood, Lady Macbeth actually helps "unmake" him, taking advantage of his weakness at a time when he most desperately depends on her. Rather than weaning him with care and thereby encouraging an individuation which both of them need, she threatens him with a severance that forces him to grip even tighter to her. [*ibid.*]

Bachmann cites an article by Barron, which includes these words: "The image in which they are to be conceived is not that of the composite personality but of a mother and son who have failed to achieve separate identities" (1960, p. 151). Freud's suggestion of the possibility of the Macbeths representing two parts of one personality is less favoured than the mother–son hypothesis.

Bachmann's description of the couple's relationship is borne out in, for example, McKellen and Dench playing the scene where Macbeth gets cold feet at the thought of murdering the king. The king and his court are dining with the Macbeths, and Macbeth leaves the table, followed swiftly by his wife, who senses something is wrong. He tries to get close to her, attempts at intervals to embrace her, to kiss her, and she pulls away and mocks him:

> . . . Art thou afeard
> To be the same in thine own act and valour
> As thou art in desire? [1(vii): 39–41]

She plays on his manhood:

> When thou durst do it, then you were a man:
> And to be more than what you were, you would
> Be so much more the man. [1(vii): 49–51]

And the powerful image of the child sucking at the breast surely threatens to emasculate him:

> . . . I have given suck, and know
> How tender 'tis to love the babe that milks me—
> I would, while it was smiling in my face,
> Have pluck'd the nipple from his boneless gums,
> And dash'd the brains out, had I so sworn
> As you have done to this. [1(vii): 54–59]

(Incidentally, this last quotation is the one that questions the childless hypothesis.)

Other psychoanalytic commentators make much of the constant appearance of father–son themes, and the necessity of Macbeth having sons to succeed him. Jekels (whose idea had influenced Freud's suggestions of the Macbeths representing two halves of one person), returned to the play in his 1933 paper. He lists the different examples: the witches say that Macbeth will become king, but Banquo will be the father of kings; Macbeth murders King Duncan, who is staying with him as his guest, the King being a supreme father figure. Macbeth is then crowned king and becomes a ruthless tyrant who orders Banquo and his son to be assassinated. A plot against Macduff's life miscarries, but his little son falls victim to Macbeth. Macduff instigates a revolt against Macbeth and kills him, and Malcolm, King Duncan's son, is made king. Jekels believes he has demonstrated "convincingly that the fundamental idea underlying this drama is the tragic realization that a bad son is a bad father, so that he thus forfeits the blessings of posterity" (*ibid.*, p. 301).

Yet the issue of children is wider than just the father–son relationship. It is essentially about having sons in the first place in order to create a succession. In a book that links the great dramatic tragedies to familial struggles and the need for immortality through issue, Bennett Simon writes:

> Lady Macbeth is never once in the text distressed about not having progeny. Her ambition is to be queen; Macbeth's ambition is to be

king, progenitor, and immortal. In my reading of the play, it is around this (literally) unspoken issue that the two begin to drift apart. [1988, p. 146]

What is seen in the play is a dramatic change in Macbeth and his wife. Freud puts it this way, wondering what might "in so short a space of time could turn the hesitating, ambitious man into an unbridled tyrant, and his steely-hearted instigator into a sick woman gnawed by remorse" (1916d, p. 322–323). One analyst, Muslin, who writes from a self-psychology perspective, sees this as occurring after the murder of King Duncan. As seen in the quotations above, Macbeth initially opposes the plan to murder the king, who is their guest, their kinsman, and a just man. Lady Macbeth dismisses her husband's argument, and in his responses, writes Muslin, we see their essential relationship: "Lady Macbeth is not just Macbeth's hardhearted ambitious wife, but rather his idealized parent. He is incapable of disobeying her, because she is revealed as the source of his strength" (1988, p. 362). After the murder, she again assumes the role of the idealized parent, calming her husband and bolstering up his resolve to follow the crime through by showing their remorse when the bodies are discovered. "Throughout these scenes", writes Muslin, "Macbeth persists in his ineptitude; he is a frightened, hesitant man in servitude to his driven mistress" (ibid.).

But, as Muslin observes, from this point onwards Macbeth is (almost) a different person. He plots to kill Banquo and his son, to murder babies (Macduff's children), and protect himself against all threats to his throne, but does this on his own initiative, without consulting his wife. He is no longer subservient to his wife on whom he had previously been dependent. "Almost" a different person, however, because there is one point when his underlying anxiety, in Muslin's words, "erupts into an episode of fragmentation and hallucination" (ibid., p. 363) when, after ordering Banquo's assassination, he hallucinates the presence of Banquo at the coronation feast. For the last time in the play, Lady Macbeth demonstrates her dominant role and tries to calm her husband through this frightening episode by reasoning with him, although her lack of success in doing that means that her role becomes that of trying to allay the anxiety of their guests:

> Sit, worthy friends. My lord is often thus,
> And hath been from his youth. Pray you, keep seat.
> The fit is momentary. [3(iii): 53–55]

In the 1997 production by Granada Television for Channel Four, directed by Michael Bogdanov (not available currently on DVD), Lady Macbeth herself appears to wilt during this scene, as if she no longer has the strength or the will to support her husband in his obvious distress. His weakness now begins to infect her. And it is not surprising, then, after the scene where Banquo's ghost appears at the feast, that she withdraws, while Macbeth's self-fragmentation leads to a state of "heightened vulnerability" (Muslin, 1988, p. 362). Without the presence of Lady Macbeth (in the language of self-psychology) as a constant self-object, Macbeth is exposed not just to real threats but to imagined threats. Lady Macbeth is no longer the leader of the two of them, and so no longer provides an idealized parental image for her husband.

So Muslin sees Macbeth as someone who suffers from a lack of real sense of self—his sense of self comes from having someone else who affirms, validates, and facilitates him. In infancy the relationship with the mother meets these functions for all of us, but where there has been a lack of such a relationship, a person may try to re-enact this early relationship in what Muslin calls "a fruitless search to complete their self-development" (*ibid.*, p. 364). The tie that someone like Macbeth makes is different from a more mature tie, where the increasing strength of the self enables the person to become relatively independent, and able to recognize and relate to an independent other. Muslin thinks Macbeth's needs are of a primitive sort; and that he requires the infusion of another to maintain his cohesiveness as a person.

Thus, writes Muslin,

> When we see Macbeth directly after the assassination of Duncan, we see a frightened and deserted man whose experience of life is profoundly altered by the separation from his leader, his spouse. He now lives in a malevolent world of his own making, a world that can be brought under control only by the extermination of any or all whom he perceives as enemies. In brief, as soon as Macbeth is without his Lady, he demonstrates the familiar manifestations of a self that has undergone a precipitous rupture from a self/

selfobject bond, and is thus suddenly subjected to anxiety and fragmentation. [*ibid.*]

In this state, Macbeth decides to seek out the three Weird Sisters in the hope that they will be able to relieve the tension in him. He tries replace the loss of Lady Macbeth with these other idealized figures, attempting to draw upon their strength in order to augment his failing sense of self-worth. As I observe below, a number of commentators in psychoanalytic literature equate the witches and Lady Macbeth as being, as they say in Scotland, "of that ilk".

Bloom, however, writing from a literary perspective, sees a rather different, though equally great, change taking place in Macbeth. Macbeth may grow more outrageous and more frightening, but his negativity, thinks Bloom, has a sublime quality. Bloom draws out the sexuality in the play, although that is of a negative kind, too. Lady Macbeth seems to taunt him in the scene referred to above where she pushes Macbeth to murder the King, as if only that way could his manliness be restored. Yet, after the murder, Bloom thinks, Macbeth turns away from his wife, and the "mutual 'greatness' they had promised each other is reduced through desexualisation" (1999, p. 529). Bloom cites Lady Macbeth's cry of "to bed, to bed" in her madness, as well as her earlier outcry, "Unsex me here". He suggests also that the terror in Macbeth is sexual in nature, "if only because murder increasingly becomes Macbeth's mode of sexual expression. Unable to beget children, Macbeth slaughters them" (*ibid.*). Bloom illustrates his thesis with a considerable number of examples of sexual imagery, including around the scene of the murder of the king, where the deed is compared to the rape of Lucrece by Tarquin in the ancient Roman myth (*ibid.*, p. 539).

Macbeth is impotent in different ways. It appears that he is unable to father children, at least in the marriage with Lady Macbeth. He is impotent as regards fate, because, as Bloom observes, although he plots incessantly, he "cannot make the drama go as he wishes. He botches it perpetually, and grows more and more outraged that his bloodiest ideas, when accomplished, trail behind them a residuum that threatens him still" (*ibid.*, p. 532).

Bloom almost eulogizes Macbeth, and perhaps in one way that is deserved, because there is indeed great beauty and poetry in many of Macbeth's speeches. Bloom believes that audiences identify with

Macbeth, even though they are nothing like him, being neither murderers nor visionaries. He suggests that we react to the play with terror, and we internalize Macbeth and his fears. Macbeth is never a secure person, and perhaps that is his appeal, because there must be a sense in which none of us is ever completely secure—we live with illusions of security. Macbeth's response to the death of Lady Macbeth is perhaps his most famous speech, and shows us something of his inner self.

> She should have died hereafter;
> There would have been a time for such a word.
> Tomorrow and tomorrow and tomorrow,
> Creeps in this petty pace from day to day
> To the last syllable of recorded time,
> And all our yesterdays have lighted fools
> The way to dusty death. Out, out, brief candle!
> Life's but a walking shadow, a poor player,
> That struts and frets upon the stage,
> And then is heard no more; it is a tale
> Told by an idiot, full of sound and fury,
> Signifying nothing. [5(v): 17–28]

It was this speech that Wilson Knight perhaps referred to when he wrote: "While Macbeth lives in conflict with himself, there is misery, evil, fear; when, at the end, he and others have openly identified himself with evil, he faces the world fearless; nor does he appear evil any longer" (cited in Bloom, 1999, p. 543). Bloom thinks he sees what Wilson Knight is aiming at: that as Macbeth moves from horror to baffled expectations, outrage takes the place of fear. Yet this is outrage at life itself, and although the speech must echo in the heart and mind of anyone who contemplates the nihilism of death, it also scorns life itself. Macbeth has not achieved that sense of reconciliation or individuation in the face of death which analysts such as, for example, Erikson or Jung clearly associate with maturity.

Antony Sher, speaking about his interpretation of Macbeth (2001), thought before rehearsals that Macbeth was just "one of Shakespeare's villains . . . a tortured soul", but he found it one of the hardest parts he had played. He sees it as a "thinking part", and he had never played anyone who thinks so much. In his study of the text he realized the contradictions in Macbeth—contradictions that are present in everyone. In Macbeth's case it was the contradiction between the soldier on the battlefield "who went beyond the call of duty", yet who later "cannot murder one old man in his own home". He in fact messes up the murder, leaves the daggers at the scene, "behaves as you and I would committing a murder". Macbeth is a "sensitive, articulate, imaginative man" who does not want to do the murder—whereas Lady Macbeth appears not to care. Freud, as explained above, thought Lady Macbeth's conscience got the better of her, but Sher suggests it is Macbeth whose conscience hurts his mind. So Sher does not see Macbeth as going mad (indeed he is very different from Lady Macbeth in the last act). He "watches himself", retains "a gruesome sanity", saying at one point, "O, full of scorpions is my mind" (3(ii): 36). He asks the doctor, albeit with reference to his wife, but perhaps also thinking of himself, "Can'st thou not minister to a mind diseas'd" (5(iii): 40). And in the "tomorrow" speech, Sher believes that Shakespeare goes on to another level, causing the actor to question even himself and the audience. The theatrical image at its close, thinks Sher, suggests the question "What are we all doing? I'm just an actor . . . What are you doing watching me?" In the stage production he came off the stage, as if it was all not worth going on with. In the film of the production, he leaves the set and goes out to the world outside. It is, as Sher says, about existential despair. (All the quotations in this paragraph come from Sher's interview, *Macbeth*, 2001.)

Yet we cannot neglect the questions that have already been raised about Lady Macbeth. There is a danger of getting too caught up on the childless theme, as the paper by Knights (1964), "How many children had Lady Macbeth?" argued. It was perhaps somewhat tongue-in-cheek, but Knights clearly thought that the pursuit of the psychological explanations about literary efforts was overdone. Calef (1969), who writes about Lady Macbeth and the question of whether or not she had had children before her marriage to Macbeth, argues that if by their explanations psychologists seek to replace literary criticism, this might be a justifiable complaint. However, some of the psychological and psychoanalytic essays about literary themes seek insights into psychological mechanisms, rather than any particular "truth" about literature and literary characters. So it is interesting, Calef believes, to ask the question whether Lady Macbeth had any children, and what happened to them; not to arrive at a quasi-historical answer, but to explore unconscious fantasies and their psychological origins and effects. A similar view is expressed from an altogether different perspective by the actor Harriet Walter, speaking about the role (*Macbeth*, 2001). She is aware that history suggests that Lady Macbeth had a child, but that theatrically the childlessness is "at the heart of the matter". Her own view is that the childlessness was a particular source of agony for both of them; and that the plot to take the throne put purpose back into the marriage, giving it a new lease of life.

Lady Macbeth's words when she is pushing Macbeth to murder the King, imply that she had had a child at some point:

> . . . I have given suck, and know
> How tender 'tis to love the babe that milks me. [1(vii): 54–55]

Yet the play also depicts quite clearly that her marriage to Macbeth was childless. For example, Macduff says, speaking of Macbeth, "He has no children" (4(iii): 217). Calef cites a personal communication where his source suggests that Lady Macbeth did have a child or children and that perhaps she had given suck only to a daughter or daughters. This source follows Jekels' idea in pointing out that the problem for the Macbeths was in the preservation of the line of continuous descent, which could only be guaranteed by sons. He points out that Macbeth failed when Banquo's son escaped, and that Macbeth's words to Lady Macbeth to "bring forth men children only" illustrate his desire for a male heir (Calef, 1969, p. 533n).

So, is there a slip here in Shakespeare's continuity? Freud, the great proponent of the slip of the pen, quotes the passage about her suckling a child, and yet does not call attention to the claims contained in Lady Macbeth's exhortation and boast, although they are not irrelevant to his thesis about the relevance of her childlessness to her mental condition.

Legend, including Shakespeare's source for the play, has it that Lady Macbeth had a child by a previous marriage, and Shakespeare might have taken it for granted that his audience would be familiar with that legend, that they knew she had been previously married, had had a child by that marriage, and that her marriage to

Macbeth was childless. The average theatre-goer today would not, of course, know that. Could Shakespeare have been concerned with the theme of childlessness and infanticide? There is little doubt that he *was* aware of Queen Elizabeth's childlessness and of the matter of the succession to the throne, which was, of course, by a Scottish king, a descendant of Banquo.

Freud's refers to Shakespeare's source, the Holinshed Chronicle, which implies that he was himself familiar with the legend. Maybe that is why he appears not to have found a paradox in the Macbeths' childlessness and Lady Macbeth's statement of having known a child at her breast, possibly because he had accepted the idea that she had had a child from a previous marriage, even though, more importantly, she remained childless with Macbeth.

Calef observes that Lady Macbeth's boast is curious, because while she says that she would be willing to murder her child to spur Macbeth on to murder Duncan, a child would help create a dynasty should she become queen. She is so desperate to become queen, that she can fantasize the murder of her child. As Calef suggests, her fantasy here is so rich and frightening that it is almost "a precursor and a premonition" of her later psychotic state: she imagines herself enjoying the pleasure of having the child at her breast and killing it (1969, p. 536). The wish to kill her child is almost unnoticed in the more powerful wish to kill the king.

Furthermore, although Lady Macbeth's ambition is murder and the establishment of a dynasty, she is unwilling to kill Duncan herself. Perhaps that is because Duncan is a surrogate father, and she cannot contemplate killing her father. For example, she says, after seeing Duncan asleep in his bed:

> Th' attempt and not the deed
> Confounds us. Hark! I laid their daggers ready;
> He could not miss them. Had he not resembled
> My father as he slept, I had done't. [2(ii): 10–13]

Yet everything she does and says in the play indicates that she wishes that her husband would kill the person who reminds her of her father, showing just how ambivalent she is. This ties in, Calef thinks, with her wish to create a dynasty with her children, yet also being willing to kill a child to do that; and this ambivalence renders

Freud's view of childlessness as punishment incomplete (Calef, 1969, p. 536).

Freud does not think the play's plot is only about ambition, and Calef thinks he is correct:

> The play is not simply explainable by the cruel ambition of a woman, more masculine than feminine. It is rather of a woman who is haunted by her love and attachment to her own father. She suffers from inner passions of which she cannot rid herself; she has to plead and urge her husband to rid her of the internal image of her father by killing an external prototype. [1969, p. 538]

It was noted above that one of Freud's suggestions about Macbeth and Lady Macbeth was that they are split characters who are not completely understandable until seen as part a single personality. Macbeth is weak-willed and acts like a feminine man. He "is goaded to brutal, fearless masculinity by his wife, while she is unsexed and becomes a masculine woman" (Blum, 1986, p. 588). This close link between them is drawn out by Freud who notes,

> It is he who has the hallucination of the dagger before the crime; but it is she who afterwards falls ill of a mental disorder . . . but we never hear that he slept no more, while the Queen . . . rises from her bed and, talking in her sleep, betrays her guilt. It is he who stands helpless with bloody hands, lamenting that "all great Neptune's ocean" will not wash them clean, while she comforts him: "A little water clears us of this deed"; but later it is she who washes her hands . . . and cannot get rid of the bloodstains: "All the perfumes of Arabia will not sweeten this little hand". Thus what he feared in his pangs of conscience is fulfilled in her; she becomes all remorse and he all defiance . . . like two disunited parts of a single psychical individuality, and it may be that they are both copied from a single prototype. [1916d, pp. 324]

Harold Blum, a New York analyst, posits a shared (what he calls a "phallic–narcissistic") fantasy in the Macbeths. They are paired as husband–wife, but unconsciously as mother–son (1986, p. 588). Lady Macbeth is the bewitching, sexually seductive mother, but she is also the incompletely separated nurturing mother. Blum is one of those who thinks she is not fully differentiated from Macbeth or from the witches. Indeed, she might even appear to be the arch witch (*ibid.*, p. 591). In much psychoanalytic writing about witches, they appear to stand for the bad mother; the mother who wants to eat the children, for example, in Hansel and Gretel, as distinct from their actual mother, who tries to get rid of them in the forest. Lady Macbeth, says Blum, is in fact "the most real and differentiated witch, the least and greatest, most benign and malignant of the witches" (*ibid.*, p. 588).

There is, then, one possibility: that the two Macbeths represent both sides of one personality. There is another explanation: that like the old weather-house figures, when one comes to the fore, the other retreats. While it is clear that to begin with Lady Macbeth is the more determined of the two, she none the less represents to Macbeth one of his own wishes, projected on to the words of the three witches at the start of the play. Harriet Walter's interview on playing the role confirms this: although she asked the director when offered the role, "Is Tony [Sher] prepared to look as if he needs me?", she is also sure that Lady Macbeth did not put the plan in Macbeth's head—she knew that he was already contemplating it (*Macbeth*, 2001).

Is it, then, that as Lady Macbeth grows more remorseful, Macbeth becomes a more hardened criminal and orders murderous attacks on his feared rivals? This is what Blum suggests (1986, p. 589). Or is it that, as she buckles under the weight of carrying them both (at the coronation feast), Macbeth loses the one person who held them together, and thrashes about for a solution, even if that solution means resorting to further murders?

As Blum says, "Lady Macbeth is an awesome figure, one of the great characters of literature" (*ibid.*, p. 590). They are not only husband and wife, but also demonstrate, as has already been noted above, a mother–son relationship, although it is of a "very special type" (*ibid.*). "He tries to cling to the passive position of the child without responsibility, directed by others and external forces" (*ibid.*, p. 592). Blum also refers to Barron (1960), who first noted that the Macbeths were not only a composite character, but that there was no ability to differentiate between them, or to achieve separate identities.

While most commentators concentrate upon the change in Lady Macbeth following the coronation feast, Blum makes an interesting observation that suggests an earlier change in her. He observes that "Lady Macbeth undergoes one of the most dramatic and terrifying transformations in literature" (*ibid.*, p. 591) much earlier in the play. This takes place, he thinks, in the scene (1(v)) where Lady Macbeth hears by letter from Macbeth about the witches' prophecy and that he has been made Thane of Cawdor. The scene contains the familiar words "the milk of human kindness" (1(v): 14), but the image of the benign breast shifts dramatically within a few lines to these words:

> . . . Come, you spirits
> That tend on mortal thoughts, unsex me here;
> And fill me, from the crown to the toe, top-full
> Of direst cruelty. Make thick my blood.
> Stop up th'access and passage to remorse,
> That no compunctious visitings of nature
> Shake my fell purpose nor keep peace between
> Th'effect and it. Come to my woman's breasts,
> And take my milk for gall, you murdering ministers . . . [1(v): 37–45]

From the milk of human kindness she rapidly shifts to the murderous mother. This makes much more sense of the later passage, already quoted above, where she again uses the image of the child at the breast to ridicule Macbeth's cowardice:

> . . . I have given suck, and know
> How tender 'tis to love the babe that milks me—
> I would, while it was smiling in my face,
> Have pluck'd the nipple from his boneless gums,
> And dash'd the brains out, had I so sworn
> As you have done to this. [1(vii): 54–59]

Blum adds that these lines sound just like child abuse and infanticide; indeed the witches echo these images later, supporting the identity between them and Lady Macbeth. They refer to "finger of birth-strangled babe" and "sow's blood that have eaten her nine farrow" (4(i): 30, 64–65) as elements in the brew they are creating in their cauldron. Blum thinks these different metaphors take us towards a deeper understanding of the drama:

Motherliness disappears, to be replaced by a devouring envy and greed. As Lady Macbeth is milked, she is depleted of nurturance and kindness; both Macbeths become mercilessly cruel. Lady Macbeth discards her conscience with her baby, although her unconscious superego will later assert itself with savage force and overpowering punishment. It is unconsciously fitting that as the instigating figure, the power behind the throne, she assumes the guilt. There is splitting between good and evil, male and female, creativity and destruction, generativity and sterility. Everything that is cruel, merciless, and murderous is associated with masculinity; everything compassionate, tender, motherly, and merciful is feminine. [1986, p. 592]

Finally, the relationship between the Macbeths contains the suggestion of a *folie à deux*. Blum refers to the term: "The rampant entitlement, seizure, and abuse of power begin as a *folie à deux*" (*ibid.*, p. 591). However, he does not really develop the idea. *Folie à deux* refers to the way in which two people act together in a way that either one would be unlikely to do on their own. They are more than joint accomplices. There is a psychological blending between two people, so that it is difficult to know who contributes what to the psychological expression of the partnership. Helene Deutsch defines the phenomenon as "the transference of delusional ideas from a person psychically ill to another person psychically healthy, who then accepts the delusional system of the ill person and assimilates it into the content of his own consciousness" (1938, p. 307). This condition might be seen as paralleled in group or mob behaviour, where many otherwise separate people seem to behave as one. Freud gives the example of hysterical manifestations involving several boarding-school girls when one of their number goes through a crisis in a blighted love affair, calling it "the mental infection" (1921c, p. 107)

Such a group situation, transient though it is in its character, bears a psychological resemblance to the more profound and continued disturbances grouped under *folie à deux*. Helene Deutsch refers to groups where psychically healthy people are carried away by psychically diseased members: world reformers and paranoiacs, for example. She says that "great national and religious movements of history and social revolutions have had, in addition to their reality motives, psychological determinants which come very close to the pathological processes of *folie à deux*" (1938, p. 307). So, in *folie à deux*, we have the psychological interplay of a group of two (Oberndorf, 1934, p. 15).

Oberndorf cites an earlier source that in *folie à deux* "there is always an infector and infectee, but neither is conscious that the influence is being exerted". He adds himself that "from the strictly technical interpretation of induced psychopathology, the inductor in neurotic familial situations is often the individual who considers himself and is often considered the normal person" (*ibid.*, p. 16).

He illustrates his article with a lengthy example (*ibid.*, pp. 17–24). A husband and wife came to him suffering from a similar symptom: she suffered a sensation of whirling whenever she left their home, and he also suffered a fear of whirling and a fear of slipping, or of his car skidding. So the two hardly ever left the house. It was impossible to work out who infected the other in the relationship, although the fear of whirling started in the husband and the wife seems to have identified with it, so much so that this symptom, which cannot be produced just by an act of will, must have been infected unconsciously. They seemed to follow one another symptomatically, so that at one stage the husband saw a surgeon because he wished to be castrated. The surgeon refused the operation, but then his wife had a sterilization through X-ray. What is also interesting is that the wife, who had been brought up a Catholic (and her husband was the son of a Protestant minister) practically abandoned her faith at the same time as her husband was converted to it. So she gave up something, but still held on to it through him.

The relationship between them seemed to indicate that the husband saw in the wife someone who was an aggressive woman, much like his own mother; and she seems to have seen in him the father whom she had never had. That in itself is not unusual in couples, that they should be attracted to each other because the other person reminds them of someone in their own family, or makes up for the lack of that kind of person in their own family. But perhaps this throws some light on *folie à deux* relationships—that what we call a *folie à deux* is a relationship where finding something in the other which one lacks then turns into a relationship where there is very little separateness. It is like when couples are first in love—in those early stages of their relationship nothing else seems to matter than each other; they feel they cannot survive without each other's presence, and cannot bear to be apart; but in time other people come back into the picture and into their lives and the two members of the couple are able to alternate between togetherness and separateness.

Helene Deutsch (1938) gives case vignettes to illustrate what she perceives as *folie à deux*. A number of similarities can be adduced from those examples:

1.   A significant figure—a parent, or parents, or perhaps a parent for one and partner for the other in the *folie à deux* pair, is missing, either because he or she has died, or is absent for some other reason like a divorce.

2.   The two people are pulled together by this absent figure, sometimes because they share common feelings about this person. They find instead the lost object in each other; or, as Oberndorf suggests about the two individuals involved in his example, both identify themselves with a lost object—the husband with a former female identification (the mother), and the wife with the lost object of male identification (presumably the father). The identifications, therefore, complement each other; and in the example many of their symptoms were mutual.

3.   The two not only come closely together, but they also cut themselves off from others—like the couple in Oberndorf's example who could not go out of the home. This may partly be because they feel that others do not share their feelings. It may also be because angry feelings towards the lost loved object are turned into paranoid feelings: other people become the angry ones, instead of them; others become angry with them, not with the lost object. But the effect is twofold:

(i).   First, the outside world is seen as more and more hostile—and it may even be in some cases that a paranoid fantasy develops, so that anyone outside the couple is seen as threatening; and this in itself pushes the couple even closer together;

(ii).   And second, there is no one then to intervene and separate the couple into their individual selves. The outside world, other people, who could actually save the couple from their *folie à deux*, are seen only as a threat, not as a means of expanding the relationship to include others, and to enable separation alongside the togetherness.

These features of *folie à deux* appear in the Macbeths: (1) they are childless; their parenting has been lost; (2) they are pulled together by their wish to create instead a dynasty; (3) their elevation to regal status cuts them off from others; and (3i) paranoid fears lead to further acts of violence, although in the case of the Macbeths this begins to push them apart; (3ii) a child would have enabled separation as well as togetherness. Although they do separate as Lady Macbeth moves in the direction of madness and suicide, we could also say that this is also the way Macbeth behaves, in his actions, though not in his poetry, becoming increasingly mad and ultimately self-destructive.

As Harriet Walter says, discussing her role as Lady Macbeth (*Macbeth*, 2001), the dynamics of the couple are very rich, and that it is by examining those dynamics that light is shed upon the play. Light is also shed on the relationships of other couples, even if less extreme in their actions than the Macbeths. The interpretations of those dynamics suggested by the writers examined in this chapter are various, and do not easily complement one another. But any one of the many interpretations may apply to couple relationships more generally, particularly when those relationships diminish rather than enhance the two partners. The Macbeths are not unique. Neither, despite the horror of their actions, are they unique in Shakespeare as a couple whose love ultimately destroys them. As the next chapter shows, Antony and Cleopatra's turbulent relationship has its own tragic consequences.

CHAPTER EIGHT

Antony and Cleopatra— "star-cross'd" lovers?

L ifting "star-cross'd lovers" from the prologue of *Romeo and Juliet* is somewhat disingenuous in the case of *Antony and Cleopatra*, and is even more so when the whole line is quoted: "A pair of star-cross'd lovers take their life". In *Romeo and Juliet* the reference is to receiving life from the procreation of two rival pairs of parents. This is no reference to suicidal actions, and indeed the deaths of Romeo and Juliet are tragic accidents of fate. But a simi- lar tragic theme pervades both plays—the love that leads to death.

Antony and Cleopatra are different—they are, for a start, older, and, one might have thought, wiser. And one of them indeed takes her life intentionally, while the other throws his life away in what may well appear to be a useless cause. He also throws away his career through his love for Cleopatra. Yet they are also "star-cross'd lovers", their love conflicting with their other roles as warrior, politician, and monarch.

The opening chapter of this book posed the question as to whether Shakespeare's characters (or at least those discussed in psychoanalytic literature) are as real as we today imagine people to be. The chapters that followed have suggested ways in which some of those characters, in the light of psychoanalytic hypotheses, may throw light upon the internal world and external relationships of ordinary people. Psychoanalytic theories are, of course, various, and in some cases apparently contradictory in interpreting those characters, but they uphold the veracity of the characters as whole persons or as part-objects. Literary scholars have argued both sides of the same question.

The criticisms made by those who think that Shakespeare's characters are not that true to life, examined, for example, in the chapter on Leontes and Othello, have also been made about the figure of Cleopatra. It is argued that the Cleopatra of the first part of the play, when Antony's fortunes are on the ascendant, is not the same woman that we see in the latter part of the play. There are, as it were, two faces, which are irreconcilable. A woman behaving as she does in the beginning of the play would not behave as she does later. The argument put forward by some critics, again referred to in Chapter One, is that Shakespeare wrote for the young nobles and the groundlings, who wanted to see blood or hear plenty of references to sex: and of course Cleopatra can be portrayed as a very sexy woman. She might be seen as more a prostitute than a queen. One of Antony's men, Enobarbus, whose role is often to comment on what he sees unfolding before him, even calls Cleopatra Antony's "Egyptian dish" (2(vi): 128)—a remarkably contemporary phrase! And Antony is called "a strumpet's fool" in Philo's opening speech (1(i): 13).

What substance is there to this argument? Antony, at one point, invites Cleopatra to wander through the streets and "note the qualities of people" (1(i): 53), a phrase cited for this book's opening chapter. So what are *her* qualities? And *his*? Is she really a whore—whose apparent change as the play proceeds makes for inconsistency in her character? And what of Anthony: do men really throw away their power for the sake of a woman? In answer to this last question, there are a number of examples of men in power, such as politicians, who fall because of an affair, sometimes even with women who appear to have been the lure in what is now called the "honey-trap". Some of those occasions depend as much on public response to scandal (greater in some cultures than in others). Yet it may be also that "star-cross'd" love renders such men less politically astute. Is that what we see here?

I draw in this chapter on the Royal Shakespeare Company's production with Richard Johnson and Janet Suzman in the title roles, directed by Trevor Nunn, now available on DVD (2004), as one of the finest performances. The opening scene shows Antony in thrall to Cleopatra. She makes him declare his love for her, to which she responds that she will set a limit on how much he can love her. When a messenger is announced and Antony does not wish to hear him, Cleopatra takes charge and admits them, at the same time mocking his relationship to his wife Fulvia. When Antony wonders what sport they shall have tonight, Cleopatra insists on hearing the ambassadors.

In a later scene, Cleopatra compares her angling in the river to the way she has caught Antony on her hook:

> . . . My bended hook shall pierce
> Their slimy jaws, and, as I draw them up,
> I'll think them every one an Antony,
> And say "Ah, ha! You're caught!" [2(v): 12–14]

Soon after this she recalls how she exchanged clothing with Antony when she had "drunk him to his bed", he wearing her head-dresses and she his sword. Only when she hears from a messenger that Antony, now back in Rome, has married his rival Octavius's sister does she appear completely disconcerted.

Combine these references with Act 1, Scene iii, where Cleopatra feigns sickness and toys with Antony's clear dilemma at having to return to Rome, examined further below, and that aspect of Cleopatra as the sexually tempting woman, enslaving Antony is very clearly stated, as well as seductively portrayed in Janet Suzman's sparkling performance of the role.

However, later, and following Antony's death, a very different Cleopatra envisages the consequences of going to Rome at Octavius's request, and how she and her maids will be treated by the officers of the law, and made figures of fun. After she has paid homage to Octavius, who has triumphed in battle over Antony and her, she addresses one of her maids about the prospect of being publicly mocked in Rome:

> . . . Saucy lictors
> Will catch at us like strumpets, and scald rhymers
> Ballad us out o' tune; the quick comedians
> Extemporally will stage us and present

> Our Alexandrian revels; Antony
> Shall be brought drunken forth; and I shall see
> Some squeaking Cleopatra boy my greatness
> I' th' posture of a whore. [5(ii): 14–19]

Either Shakespeare is being supremely bold here in mocking his own play and the boy playing the lead as Cleopatra, or he is saying through Cleopatra that she is not of that type at all, and that it would be torturous for her to be mocked in this way. So is there an inconsistency?

J. I. M. Stewart, who argues in *Character and Motive in Shakespeare* that Shakespeare was writing from a sound knowledge of human nature, departs at this point from the support he usually finds in Freud. Instead, he puts forward what we might call now a social constructionist argument: that what we call "human nature" is "shaped . . . by the system of proprieties operative in the culture to which we belong" (1949, p. 69). We tend to assess, or even judge, people by how well they either fit or do not fit the social norms of a particular culture. And, as Stewart says, "cultures differ widely in their conceptions of human nature . . . behaviour which in the opinion of those within a culture is perfectly consistent may appear wildly inconsistent to an observer from without" (*ibid.*, p. 70). Stewart gives a number of examples from different native cultures, and then suggests that what people think about a woman who has wide erotic experience will vary between communities according to their varying social ideologies. Within any one culture most people conform to the norm, although some express their individuality more strongly.

This may lead to two forms of argument, which should not be confused. It is possible to see Cleopatra as highly individualistic, refusing to conform to the expectations of her own society; or preferably, and what is perhaps the stronger argument, that while within certain societies at certain times it might be held that an erotic woman cannot also be a strong woman or a major political force, in other societies it could be very different. A different example from that time is that it was the custom in Egyptian culture for brother and sister to marry, as Cleopatra was married to her brother Ptolemy XIII, although the marriage was essentially symbolic and not consummated sexually. That would certainly not be the custom in many other societies. And Egypt had several strong women in its historic dynasties.

While Shakespeare was writing this play, some three years after the death of Elizabeth I, the memory of that strong political woman may not have been far from his mind. Whether or not the virgin queen was also wildly erotic is much more debatable, since we have no privileged view of her bedchamber or of her behaviour with her supposed lovers. Furthermore, we need to take into account that Stewart is writing in the late 1940s, when attitudes to women were probably much more of the sort which those critics of the character of Cleopatra put forward. Women were either erotic objects, or they were mothers, or they were on occasion intellectually and politically strong—politically much less so than now, although intellectually women were beginning to be seen as the equals of men. Yet such women were hardly seen as erotic. Freud, for example, writing only a few years earlier, referred to some of "our excellent women colleagues" (1933d, p. 116) researching female psychology: when they say to their male colleagues that they are prejudiced against women, his reply is "this doesn't apply to you. You're the exception; on this point you're more masculine than feminine" (*ibid.*, p. 116–117)!

If these repressive views of woman predominated in the minds of these critics, then of course a strong woman, as in the second part of Cleopatra, could not possibly also be erotic. The two did not go together. Sex, at least for women, dissipated intelligence. As Stewart comments,

> In our society a sensually uncontrolled woman is potentially more disruptive than a sensually uncontrolled man, and as a consequence different behaviour-patterns and systems of expectation are built up for the two sexes. A man may have many mistresses and nobody will think to say he "exercises a trade" simply on the strength of his exploiting his sexual attractiveness to gain sexual gratification . . . nor . . . is such a man be judged markedly incapable of fidelity or less likely than another to show "fortitude" when adversity comes. [1949, p. 72]

But for a woman, at the time Stewart was writing, it is a quite different case—"more odium attaches to her change of troth, any ultimate fidelity is supposed to be beyond her reach" (*ibid.*).

One of the critics Stewart argues against, Professor Schücking (1922), categorizes Cleopatra as a whore in the first part of the play and as a thoughtful and motherly woman in the second part—and then proceeds to argue that she is not a real character because these two Cleopatras cannot be one and the same person.

Freud, as we might suspect from the reference above, has the same difficulty as Stewart's Germanic opponent; not about Cleopatra, but about the psychology and character of women. He writes about a different topic, but he suggests that the different developmental paths through the Oedipus complex result in the formation of different types of superego in men and women. In a paper on "Some psychical consequences of the anatomical distinction between the sexes", he writes,

> I cannot evade the notion (though I hesitate to give it expression) that for women the level of what is ethically normal is different from what it is in men. Their super-ego is never so exorable, so impersonal, so independent of its emotional origins as we require it to be in men. Character-traits which critics of every epoch have brought up against women—that they show less sense of justice than men, that they are less ready to submit to the great exigencies of life, that they are more often influenced in their judgments by feelings of affection and hostility—all these would be amply accounted for by the modification in the formation of their super-ego. [1925j, pp. 257–258]

If women are more emotional in the way they make decisions, pass judgement, etc. (that is the women who are not "more male than female"!), we are only a short way from the argument that their sense of political judgement cannot be as pure as men's; or, in the case of Cleopatra, she cannot rise to the heights of fortitude and bravery as a man might.

Psychological differences between the sexes is an interesting subject both for research and for debate. Carol Gilligan (1982) has researched the way women make moral judgements, following similar research by Kohlberg (1981), which put forward research evidence that men were more highly developed in their moral judgements than women. Gilligan argues that men and women have different conceptions of morality—that men focus on justice, fairness, rules, and rights, whereas women emphasize people's wants, needs, interests, and aspirations.

Yet, if there are differences between men and women, elsewhere Freud writes as if he wants to reject the attempts of the early feminists to blur differences. He challenges the assumption that character differences in men and women should be based upon such terms as "active" and "passive". In the same paper where he praises his women colleagues as being more like men, he argues that psychologically there need be no difference between men and women, and that to call men active and women passive is purely a social convention (1933a, pp. 114–117); so we find him preceding Stewart's social constructionism, when he writes "we must be aware . . . of underestimating the influence of the social customs, which similarly force women into passive situations" (1933/2003, p. 115).

And much earlier, in a paper in 1908, Freud draws attention to the double standards in society in relation to sexual morality. Put plainly, he says that men get away with breaking the strict moral code relating to abstinence from sex outside marriage—but that women are not permitted to. Stewart, as indicated above, echoes such an argument. Furthermore, Freud writes of attitudes at the time that "if a man is energetic in winning the object of his love, we are confident that he will pursue his other aims with an equally unswerving energy" (1908c, p. 198). Sexual prowess appears to signify prowess in other spheres of life, too. But for a woman, he says, the same equation applies, but in reverse. To take an intellectual interest in sexual problems is seen "as unwomanly and a sign of a sinful disposition" (*ibid.*, p. 198). Women have extreme inherent curiosity, suggests Freud, but such curiosity is condemned in a woman. It would be easy to read his next sentence the wrong way-but, in fact, again Freud is supporting this equation of character and social construction: "I think that the undoubted intellectual inferiority of so many woman can rather be traced back to the inhibition of thought necessitated by sexual suppression" (*ibid.*, p. 199). In other words, if women appear to be less intellectually confident, it is because society has suppressed them in many other ways, including in respect of their sexual confidence.

It was, of course, 100 years ago when Freud was writing this. And it is a half-century since Stewart was writing about Cleopatra in this vein. Stewart is arguing against critics mainly writing within that fifty-year period before his book. It would not be surprising, therefore, if Cleopatra were to be viewed differently today, although it remains questionable whether women have yet been liberated from the social conventions that make it difficult for them to be both erotic and determined, political, intelligent, brave, and all the other qualities which Cleopatra shows.

There is another way of approaching the apparent contradictions in Cleopatra's character. Murray Cox and Alice Theilgaard, in their book *Shakespeare as Prompter*, use Cleopatra as an example of it being absurd to think in terms of the right diagnostic formulation of her personality structure (1994, p. 182). We have to look at both the surface and the depth of people. Their judgement is that Cleopatra "manifests a wide range of behavioural features seen in varying proportions in a routine psychiatric out-patient clinic"— although of course such a sentence pathologizes her unduly, suggesting she is psychiatrically ill. They maintain that Shakespeare challenges us to focus upon and be attentive to what people present—the implication there being that people do not necessarily fit standard textbooks. What Shakespeare does, as any good dramatist or novelist also does, is to increase our awareness of human nature and extend our understanding of the qualities of people.

Cox and Theilgaard also cite a personal communication in which Vivian Thomas said of Antony and Cleopatra that "many critical incidents . . . are not amenable to unequivocal interpretations", which they say is just as true of ordinary life (*ibid.*, p. 19). Harold Bloom, too, observes that critics can never agree very much about Cleopatra, since she is, of all Shakespeare's representations of woman, "the most subtle and formidable . . . the audience is given an enigmatic range of possible judgements and interpretations" (1999, p. 546). This is a warning, not just to the literary critic and commentator, but also, as seen in Cox and Theilgaard, to psychiatrists, psychologists, and therapists, not to think that there is only one way of interpreting and understanding character and behaviour. It is the danger of the label in psychiatry, which, being so medically based, tends to seek definitive terms to match those of physical medicine. Cleopatra is complex—as any other person is complex.

So, we may need to approach Cleopatra from alternative perspectives. That does not mean dismissing either her erotic nature, or her strong fortitude. Indeed, something of her strength is seen in the way she can use her eroticism to keep Antony "hooked".

As a politician she perhaps knew what she wished to gain from this relationship, possibly using her sexuality to do that; but she was also changed by the relationship.

One feature of her complex personality is her narcissism—her "extreme narcissism", as Cox and Theilgaard put it (1994, p. 367), citing Act 2(ii): 216: "even the air has gone to gaze on Cleopatra". Bloom calls her "the archetype of the star, the world's first celebrity", and comments that "Cleopatra never stops acting the part of Cleopatra" (1999, p. 548)—this may be one way of interpreting her wish for her robe and crown when she commits suicide. If we ask what the nature of the relationship is between Antony and Cleopatra, we may wonder whether they really are in love with each other, as Bloom asks (*ibid.*, p. 549) or whether it is actually mutual fascination—twinned narcissism. There is, as discussed below, a twinned fantasy. The two lovers seem to feed off each other, as one might expect of a narcissistic couple, rather than expand each other's possibilities.

Stewart concludes his discussion of Cleopatra by asserting that poetry is the key to her character (1949, p. 73). She may be "a woman absorbed in the mystery of sensuality. But that for her sensuality *is* a mystery, and not a trade, is shown by the poetry in which she spontaneously clothes it" (*ibid.*, pp. 73–74, original emphasis). This is as true of her at the beginning of the play (he suggests that Shakespeare would not have had a harlot speak such poetry) as it is at the end, and "in her great moments, in fact, Cleopatra says things very characteristic of her earlier self" (*ibid.*, p. 74), although she is also changed.

Towards the end of the play, says Stewart, there is still something of the old rage, but "our preponderant impression is of a woman who has achieved an unexpected spiritual stature" (*ibid.*, p. 75). So, while she may appear at the start as a "wanton" woman, sunk in sensuality, the poetry she speaks suggests something else in her character, which is the essence of her, the "truth of her". In Stewart's words, "Through her sterile sensuality there has subterraneously run the quickening stream; and here at last in her monument . . . like water cleaving the rock, her womanhood discloses itself in a mature and final splendour" (*ibid.*).

Her death is, seen on stage or screen, splendid—crowned and robed she applies the asp to her breast, and dies alongside her maids:

Give me my robe. Put on my crown. I have
Immortal longings in me. Now no more
The juice of Egypt's grape shall moist this lip.
. . . Quick! Methinks I hear
Antony call. I see him rouse himself
To praise my noble act. I hear him mock
The luck of Caesar, which the gods give men
To excuse their after wrath. Husband, I come!
Now to that name my courage prove my title!
I am fire and air; my other elements
I give to baser life. [5(ii): 278–288]

But, asks Stewart, is this just conventional Hollywood fiction? Is it like the silver screen, where we are weeping into a handkerchief at the end of the film, but come out into the cold air to feel cheated by some "counterfeit of human passion" (1949, p. 77). Or, we might add, is this just narcissistic fantasy? Stewart's answer is to the contrary:

We are convinced of a profound significance in what we have witnessed. And we may assert—contemplating still the close of the play—that our impression of truth in the fable results not from an illusion which the poetry creates but from an actual correlation between high dramatic poetry and insight into substantial human nature. [*ibid.*]

He concludes that Cleopatra "contrives her own heroism, exploiting an exotic and womanly ritual of robe and crown to dredge up attitudes and potencies that ordinarily lie sunk and obscured below her grasp" (*ibid.*, pp. 77–78).

The discussion of Cleopatra has, up to this point, been dominated by the literary critics, even if they, too, sometimes draw upon psychoanalytic ideas. There is only one sustained examination of Cleopatra in the psychoanalytic journals, although she is referred to several times, mainly in the context of clinical vignettes of patients who have the fantasy of being Cleopatra, someone who is potent, admired, and dominant.

For example, in an article titled "Delusion, fantasy and desire", Lichtenberg and Pao describe Mrs B, who spoke of herself in several sessions running as having been a very beautiful woman, with young men and her husband catering for her needs. She had enjoyed ordering these men around. Her husband gave her the nickname "princess" and called her the "Queen of Sheba". She recalled that her favourite game between the ages of seven and ten years was pretending to be Cleopatra, wearing one of her mother's dresses and a paper crown, and commanding the obedience of children in the neighbourhood as her subjects. A few years before her therapy, in a psychotic episode, Mrs B had declared that she was Cleopatra, and as Cleopatra she wanted all her demands fulfilled instantly. If this did not happen, she flew into a rage. She would imperiously order anyone who refused to meet her demands to get out of her sight and not come before her again, otherwise she would order their death. She was so convinced of who she was that she would say that they had better not forget that it was Cleopatra with whom they were dealing (Lichtenberg and Pao, 1974, p. 273).

Here, indeed, we see the grandiosity and primary narcissism of the baby; "His Majesty the Baby", as Freud termed it (1914c, p. 91), and as linked in Chapter Four to Lear. Others (particularly mother) are initially there to fulfil all the baby's needs and demands. Lichtenberg and Pao comment that "Mrs B's Cleopatra delusion expressed the intensity of her unfulfilled need to be reassured that she was worthy of the presence, the nurture, and the sharing of power of the mother–child dyad" (1974, p. 276). One of these two authors may be citing the same case in an earlier article, where he refers to an in-patient who, believing herself to be Cleopatra, considered her word as law. She could fly into a rage, and would, in such a state, often say, "I can kill you", but "when not provoked she acted as if she were flooded with love, despite the fact that she looked extremely angry" (Pao, 1968, p. 817). She portrayed herself as someone who was extremely full of love and energy.

An interesting aside for those familiar with the history of psychoanalysis, as the letters of James and Alix Strachey show, is that Melanie Klein, perhaps the grandest and most powerful of women analysts, and in the eyes of some on a par with Freud, loved to attend dances with her friend Alix in her favourite costume dressed as Cleopatra (Meisel & Kendrick, 1985)!

There is one article in the psychoanalytic journals that is solely devoted to the play. Janis Krohn examines "The dangers of love in Antony and Cleopatra", in which he raises some interesting questions about the nature of love—or perhaps the nature of passion. He writes not about mature love, but a type of love in a mature couple, in this case Antony and Cleopatra, a love which destroys them both. He observes first that it is rare to find mature loving couples in Shakespeare—they are either young, as seen mainly in the comedies, or they are tragic relationships, where we see little sign of actual love in the two partners and which end in premature death. Macbeth and Lady Macbeth might be the only other mature couple we see in a close loving relationship, although the principal theme there is hardly their love—more, as we saw in Chapter Seven, their struggle for power and progeny, perhaps, as suggested there, to try and keep alive their love.

Antony and Cleopatra provides, Krohn writes, "a unique opportunity to see how Shakespeare perceived and portrayed the tensions of an established love" (1986, p. 89). The relationship is portrayed as fated, so that although they try to honour their commitment to each other, it is threatened by external events that appear to be the cause of the destruction of their love. However, these external events mirror in some sense the internal dangers to their relationship: "The real tragedy of Antony and Cleopatra lies not in their failure to surmount difficulties posed by the external situation; rather, the tragedy lies in their inability to overcome the internal conflicts and fears posed in their relationship" (*ibid.*). Fantasized dangers, which represent hidden conflicts, destroy their relationship. Krohn observes that their fantasies are not unusual; they are often encountered in clinical work—but in understanding these fantasies we may be able to see why Antony and Cleopatra are unable to attain lasting contentment for themselves, and why their suicides do not leave the audience with the same type of feelings as the other Shakespearean tragedies.

The description of Antony as a "strumpet's fool" (1(i): 13), occurs in Philo's opening words, where he says what has gone wrong in Antony: that in his love for Cleopatra he has become immoderate, and is no longer a great general and great man. Antony's passion has led to the diminishing of his manhood, particularly in battle and in politics. Krohn observes that this view is shared by Antony, whose passion pushes him towards, and yet pulls him away from, Cleopatra. The reason for this "push–pull" is that the more he is in love, the more he fears he must give up his manhood. "The more he loves her, the less he is a man" (Krohn, 1986, p. 90). This is the major fantasy, which, along with its variations, appears throughout the play.

The opening scene has already been described above, where Antony, even if Cleopatra urges otherwise, refuses to admit the messenger from Rome. Instead of remaining as he was, an important politician, a significant figure in the Roman world, he wants to embrace Cleopatra, and plan what they should do together that night. The playful conversation between Antony and Cleopatra shows them jostling for position, "as if it is as important to prevail over the other as it is to feel close" (*ibid.*). Antony, as shown above, has become a plaything, someone whom Cleopatra toys with, while for his part he appears to be completed besotted with her. In a manner which is more playful, but none the less as powerful as Lady Macbeth, she uses shame and guilt to persuade her man to do what his conscience makes him hesitant to do. Although there is a power struggle between the two lovers, there is also a struggle within Antony, since the danger of being in love is that he becomes totally emotionally dependent upon the other. It is true that Krohn draws attention to Cleopatra's wiles, but he actually concentrates upon Antony's responses, and how Antony cannot hold together both his passion (his adopted Egyptian self) and his political position (his Roman self). There is a parallel position here to that discussed above, where some critics hold that Cleopatra cannot be both passionate lover and a political strong woman. Antony clearly has to struggle with this conflict, making this another possibility in interpreting Cleopatra, that she, too, has these two sides to her, perhaps rather more successfully using one side (passion) to promote the other side of her (the political). Yet what is also argued is that in the struggle between these two sides, whether it is in the man or the woman, it is difficult, or in this play perhaps impossible, to hold the two together.

The internal struggle within Antony is seen, as Krohn observes, at the point where he is told of his wife Fulvia's death. For the moment he feels guilty, and appears to intend ending the relationship with Cleopatra:

> The present pleasure,
> By revolution lowering, does become

> The opposite of itself: she's good, being gone,
> The hand could pluck her back that shov'd her on.
> I must from this enchanting queen break off,
> Ten thousand harms, more than the ills I know,
> My idleness doth hatch. [1(ii): 121–127]

He knows that Cleopatra enchants him; he senses, too, perhaps, that he is being tempted along a path that could lead to self-destruction. In a moment of insight, he sees that he should break free from her enchantments.

But in the next scene (Act 1(iii)) his determination soon melts. The struggle for dominance in the relationship between Antony and Cleopatra is again starkly seen: Cleopatra uses her guile again, putting on a play to entrance and entrap Antony. She says coyly and, of course, deceptively, "I have no power upon you" (1(iii): 23), but in saying this, she uses powerful phrases to persuade Antony to remain with her:

> I am sick and sullen. (1(iii): 13)

> Pray you, stand farther from me. (1(iii): 17)

> Let her not say 'tis I that keep you here—
> I have no power upon you. (1(iii): 22–33)

> But bid farewell, and go. When you sued staying,
> Then was the time for words. No going then!
> Eternity was in our lips and eyes,
> Bliss in our brows' bent, none our parts so poor
> But was a race of heaven. They are so still,
> Or thou, the greatest soldier in the world,
> Art turn'd the greatest liar. (1(iii): 33–38)

> Sir, you and I must part—but that's not it.
> Sir, you and I have lov'd—but that's not it.
> That you know well. Something it is I would -
> O, my oblivion is a very Antony,
> And I am all forgotten. (1(iii): (87–91)

Cleopatra tugs at his heart strings, line after line, pulling him, pushing him away, until he cannot but bow to her blandishments.

So, Krohn argues, we build up a picture of a man who is emasculated by his love for the woman, as indeed Octavius describes Antony early in the play, who

> . . . is not more manlike
> Than Cleopatra; nor the queen of Ptolemy
> More womanly than he: hardly gave audience, or
> Vouchsaf'd to think he had partners. [1(iv): 5–8]

And later Agrippa refers to Cleopatra as taking away Antony's sword—a wonderful image of castration!:

> Royal wench!
> She made great Caesar lay his sword to bed;
> He plough'd her, and she cropp'd. [2(ii): 227–228]

Krohn writes, "Antony has become more like a woman than a man—castrated and having abdicated his role in world leadership and abandoned his male partners (1986, p. 91).

Yet Cleopatra is also a major player, not just a seductive woman. She has needs, too, not just the wish to dominate. She delights in her "demi-Atlas of this earth" (1(v): 23). Antony is powerfully significant for her because he demonstrates, when she first meets him, virility and manliness. She loves him above all because he represents for her what it is to be a man. Therefore, there arises a deep tension for the two of them, which Krohn summarizes well. The conflict that exists for them both is that the more Antony loves Cleopatra the less a man does he become, and yet this is precisely what Cleopatra wants from him, this representation of masculinity. Thus, it is a doomed relationship from the start, because what each wants leads to them both having nothing. Cleopatra wants Antony's masculinity; he loses his masculinity the more he submits to her; she then does not get what she wants since he is no longer the man she loves.

Cleopatra's fantasy does not match the reality of what their relationship is doing to Antony. But even if much of the language points to Antony becoming less of a man in her eyes—it cannot be overlooked that with his death her love seems as strong, if not stronger than ever. Perhaps that is because at least in battle he proved his bravery again, even if he lost. Perhaps it is because her fantasy can flower when there is no reality to hold it in check. She can idealize him, instead of struggle with the reality of their doomed relationship. Bloom remarks (1999, p. 565) that some commentators think that Cleopatra is only in love with Antony when he is dead, although Bloom is of the opinion that her devotion to Antony does not touch its height until he dies in her arms.

In Act 2, Agrippa proposes that Antony weds Octavia, Octavius's sister, since this will bind the men closer together. "Cleopatra is contrasted with Octavia—Cleopatra pulls Antony away from relationships with men, particularly Caesar, while Octavia is to provide a pathway between Antony and Caesar" (Krohn, 1986, p. 92). The problem is that Antony is not in love with Octavia. Antony also learns through the soothsayer that he will not get what he seeks from his relationship with Octavius: his manliness is threatened in a different way, in a competition with Octavius, the younger man. Krohn observes that "faced with failure vis-à-vis the powerful man, he returns to the beloved woman" (ibid.).

This conflict between love of women and losing manliness, as Krohn illustrates, occurs time and again in the play. Act 3 dramatizes the dilemma further: "If a man loves too much, he loses his honour because he cannot leave his woman's sphere. But then, he is no good to her because he is castrated" (ibid.). The danger that women pose for men is made explicit, often in remarks by Enobarbus:

> If we should serve with horse and mares together,
> The horse were merely lost; the mares would bear
> A soldier and his horse. [3(vii): 7–9]

And a little later in the same scene, Canidius says: "So our leader's led, and we are women's men" (3(vii): 69–70).

This is seen most graphically when, in the battle at sea, Antony does not stay to fight, but follows Cleopatra's ship away from the battle, thereby both losing the battle and abandoning his honour and manhood. Of this foolish demonstration of his concern for her, one of his men says:

> She once being loof'd,
> The noble ruin of her magic, Antony,
> Claps on his sea-wing, and, like a doting mallard,
> Leaving the fight in height, flies after her:
> I never saw an action of such shame;
> Experience, manhood, honour, ne'er before
> Did violate so itself. [3(x): 18–24]

Or, as Krohn comments, "With this action, Antony becomes finally and completely Cleopatra's 'fool'—her phallus to be used as she wishes, no longer owned or possessed exclusively by himself" (1986, p. 93). Antony indeed appears at first to be full of shame, and he expresses anger both with himself and towards Cleopatra. But even that does not last for long, because when Cleopatra begs his forgiveness (and we may wonder again whether she is putting on a clever act), Antony quickly pardons her, and (believe it or not!) even calls for wine and food as if he wants to celebrate despite all their misfortunes.

In this fascinating article Krohn therefore argues that the major underlying fantasy in this play, is "that a woman will lead a man to surrender his virility and ultimately leave him castrated as a consequence of his love for her" (*ibid.*); but there is as well a "parallel fantasy about men" that by contact with another man a man can regain his strength and confirm the possession of the phallus—in the same way as psychoanalytic theory supposes that a boy uses identification with his father to develop a sense of manhood. Krohn argues that this is partly why, after the defeat at sea, Antony proposes having a man-to-man fight with Octavius. Krohn cites these lines as evidence that after fighting Octavius Antony will replenish his masculinity and become a complete man again:

ANTONY: Dost thou hear, lady?
            If from the field I shall return once more
            To kiss these lips, I will appear in blood,
            I, and my sword, will earn our chronicle:
            There's hope in't yet.

To which Cleopatra replies (as if like a mother to a son!),

            That's my brave lord! [3(xiii): 172–177]

Cleopatra proceeds to help him on with his armour, which Krohn thinks is an ambiguous image: "She could be womanizing the act of a man putting on his armour, or she could be helping Antony regain his masculinity through the gesture of putting on the armour" (1986, p. 93). Antony is this time victorious in battle, and feels powerful once more, although it is difficult to see quite where Krohn finds his evidence for saying that this moment is "a peak in

134 SHAKESPEARE ON THE COUCH

their experience of love for each other" (*ibid.*, p. 94) because, as he says, the moment does not last.

The see-saw struggle between parts of himself goes on. Antony is once more defeated in battle and blames Cleopatra. Here Krohn writes,

> If we have been understanding the components and fantasies contained in Antony's love for Cleopatra correctly, then his rage is triggered not just because he feels she is lost to him, but also because he feels she has implicitly taken with her his phallus. [*ibid.*]

Once more Cleopatra puts on an act. She tries to mollify Antony by forcing him back to her side, sending a message that she has committed suicide, hoping that this will make him feel guilty. To an extent she succeeds, although Antony's response is not the one she expected, because the news leads him to want to die himself. His masculinity seems undermined yet further when his suicide attempt is bungled. He is brought to Cleopatra, discovers, of course, that she is not dead, and dies in her arms. His dying words, his final speech, appear to signify both contentment and sorrow: there is a type of resolution (even if literally short-lived) in that Antony is reunited with his lover, and at the same time believes that in his death he has died as a man:

> The miserable change now at my end
> Lament nor sorrow at; but please your thoughts
> In feeding them with those my former fortunes
> Wherein I liv'd: the greatest prince o' th' world,
> The noblest; and do now not basely die,
> Not cowardly put off my helmet to
> My countryman—a Roman, by a Roman
> Valiantly vanquish'd. [4(xv): 51–58]

Yet we may also wonder whether his death is actually a satisfactory resolution, even if it was almost inevitable. Death, as in Cleopatra's phrase "the soldier's pole is fallen", is perhaps the ultimate emasculation.

Psychoanalysis might, of course, be criticized for promoting the idea of the castrating woman, and in some respects, even if corrected by its own feminist critics, attempting to reinforce the need for man to retain power over the threat of woman. Krohn is a little more sympathetic, rejecting the *vagina dentata* idea in relation to Cleopatra (1986, p. 93), and suggesting that in the final Act Cleopatra achieves a kind of resolution, too, when she recounts a dream:

> I dream't there was an Emperor Antony . . .
> His legs bestrid the ocean; his rear'd arm
> Crested the world: his voice was propertied
> As all the tuned spheres, and that to friends;
> But when he meant to quail, and shake the orb,
> He was as rattling thunder . . . [5(ii): 76, 82–88]

Krohn believes that in this dream Cleopatra takes into herself an Antony, a giant like Atlas, "a quintessentially phallic man" (1986, p. 95). Psychoanalytic theories have suggested that the figures in a dream are part of the self; in this dream therefore she shares in his fantasized phallic prowess—it is a part of herself. Similarly, by joining Antony in her own suicide, she acts out the fantasy of joining herself to his phallic power forever. For her suicide she uses an asp, which is a classic Freudian phallic symbol. She names it her "fool", and this word echoes the first scene of the play when Antony is called the "strumpet's fool", and, as Krohn says, the two lovers struggled with the issue of who was going to be the fool to whom (*ibid.*).

Unfortunately, despite stating early on in his article that the fantasies in their relationship are seen in clinical work, Krohn does not give any clinical examples of the fantasy of the man who is emasculated by his love for a woman, and of the woman's fantasy of wanting a manly man, who is then disappointed by the man succumbing to her and so losing his masculinity. Is it therefore true of some couples? Nevertheless, the observation made above of the parallel situations, whether Cleopatra can be both a sexual woman and a powerful woman, and whether Antony can be passionate lover and a powerful man, poses an interesting question. Can such a relationship survive? Krohn suggests that if they had not committed suicide, Antony's and Cleopatra's relationship would not have lasted. Their failure to resolve the issue—except in heroic death—perhaps constitutes something of the tragedy of the play. It is a tragedy that lacks the depth of *King Lear, Hamlet, Macbeth,* and *Othello.* But if one of the elements of tragedy is the struggle with the consequences of action or inaction, it is a play that has distinct similarities to the four great tragedies. The lesser tragedies of more ordinary relationships are no less painful for all that.

There are, of course, many relationships where the "power" balance between the couple works well; where each complements the other without detracting from the other. In *Antony and Cleopatra* it seems that it is the passion, and the constant attempts to rekindle that passion, which marks the downfall of the couple, both individually and together. Fantasy exists in all relationships, but more so at their start than later on. It is when fantasy gives way to reality that the true mettle of a relationship is revealed; and at such times some relationships break, while others change—shifting the emphasis without losing altogether the initial reason for the attraction. Antony's and Cleopatra's relationship did not change, but seesawed over the years until the breaking point was triggered by external events. Who knows what might have happened if Octavius had not constituted a threat to Egypt and their relationship? But even in imagination of such an event, we might suspect that each of them would have had to change for their relationship to survive.

CHAPTER NINE

Epilogue

And the rest . . .?

There are of course other characters in Shakespeare who might merit the type of examination given to those discussed in previous chapters. Psychoanalytic writing includes a scattering of references to some of those who come to mind—Richard II, Richard III, Titus Andronicus, even the narcissistic Malvolio—but there is not generally the interest in them that has been generated in the characters examined here.

Yet Hamlet? "Ay, there's the rub!" (*Hamlet*, 3(i): 65). That is a completely different picture, and the reader may wonder why there is not a chapter devoted to him within these covers.

The answer is that there are so many articles and books interpreting Hamlet that it is impossible in a single chapter to do either him or psychoanalysis justice. He merits a book to himself, as indeed (referring back to my Prologue) when teaching "Shakespeare on the couch", nearly the whole of my second course was given over to his play.

Hamlet takes us into the whole question raised by Freud, and pursued in Freud's defence by Ernest Jones (1949), of the Oedipal issues that may have been behind his inability to exact revenge for

137

his father's apparent murder. But, if for some it is the Oedipus myth that helps us unpack his dilemma, for others it is the Orestes myth. Other analysts have challenged the Freud–Jones view, and suggested alternative reasons for Hamlet's inability to act. Apart from the problem of parricide there is the question of matricidal wishes, which may also be present; there are issues of intergenerational conflict, of parental watchfulness and interfering oversight, not just in Hamlet's case, but with regard to Ophelia too. There is much in the way the women in the play—Gertrude and Ophelia—can themselves be understood. Some writing has discussed the mutuality of the Oedipus complex in relation to Gertrude, Hamlet's mother. Ophelia is of immense interest, too: apart from Hamlet's ambivalent relationship to her, there have been discussions in psychoanalytic literature of what drove her mad. In addition, there is the question of Hamlet's madness, and whether it was feigned or not; and if it was feigned what the effect of his role-playing madness might have been, both on Hamlet and on the way others treated him. There is the trickery of the play within the play, which itself leads to speculation about its link to dreaming within dreams. There is speculation, too, about the role of the trickster and Hamlet, and of the shape-shifting figure.

It is immediately apparent that such rich speculation could not be encompassed within a single chapter; and indeed others have written more authoritatively and fluently on psychoanalysis and Hamlet than the present author might. So for that reason, in Hamlet's final, dying, words (at least as far as this book is concerned):

The rest is silence (5(ii): 363).

REFERENCES

Aarons, Z. A. (1970). Normality and abnormality in adolescence—with a digression on Prince Hal "The sowing of wild oats". *Psychoanalytic Study of the Child, 25*: 309–339.

Alexander, B. (1920). *Shakespeare*. Budapest: Franklin.

Alexander, F. (1933). A note on Falstaff. *Psychoanalytic Quarterly, 2*: 592–606.

Antony and Cleopatra (2004). The Royal Shakespeare Company, directed by Trevor Nunn, with Richard Johnson and Janet Suzman. Available on DVD: B000223QM (currently Region 1 only).

Anzieu, D. (1984). *The Group and the Unconscious*. London: Routledge and Kegan Paul.

Bach, R. A. (1999). Antonio and Bassanio. *Journal of the American Psychoanalytic Association, 47*: 573–580.

Bachmann, S. (1978). "Daggers in men's smiles"—the "truest issue" in *Macbeth*. *International Review of Psycho-Analysis, 5*: 97–104.

Barron, D. (1960). The babe that milks: an organic study of *Macbeth*. *American Imago, 17*: 133–161.

Bloom, H. (1999). *Shakespeare: The Invention of the Human*. London: The Fourth Estate.

Blum, H. P. (1986). Psychoanalytic studies and Macbeth—shared fantasy and reciprocal identification. *Psychoanalytic Study of the Child, 41*: 585–599.

Boswell, J. (2000). Review of *The Uninvited Guest: Emerging from Narcissism towards Marriage*. *International Journal of Psychoanalysis, 81*: 1039–1041.

Bradley, A. C. (1909). The rejection of Falstaff. In: A. C. Bradley, *Oxford Lectures on Poetry*. London: Macmillan [reprinted by Atlantic Books].

Brown, J. R. (1959). (Ed.). *The Merchant of Venice*. Arden Edition of the Works of Shakespeare. Cambridge: Harvard University Press.

Calef, V. (1969). Lady Macbeth and infanticide or "How many children had Lady Macbeth" murdered? *Journal of the American Psychoanalytic Association*, 17: 528–548.

Coriat, I. H. (1921). Anal–erotic character traits in Shylock. *International Journal of Psychoanalysis*, 2: 354–360.

Cox, M. (Ed.) (1992). *Shakespeare Comes to Broadmoor*. London: Jessica Kingsley.

Cox, M. and Theilgaard, A. (1994). *Shakespeare as Prompter: The Amending Imagination and the Therapeutic Process*. London: Jessica Kingsley.

Deutsch, H. (1938). Folie à deux. *Psychoanalytic Quarterly*, 7: 307–318.

Donnelly, J. (1953). Incest, ingratitude and insanity: aspects of the psychopathology of King Lear. *Psychoanalytic Review*, 40: 149–155.

Erikson, E. (1965). *Childhood and Society*. London: Penguin.

Faber, M. D. (1967). Oedipal patterns in Henry IV. *Psychoanalytic Quarterly*, 36: 426–434.

Fisher, J. V. (1999). *The Uninvited Guest: Emerging from Narcissism towards Marriage*. London: Karnac.

Fleisher, M. L. (1999). Shylock and Antonio's bond. *Journal of the American Psychoanalytic Association*, 47: 551–571.

Fliess, R. (1956). *Erogenicity and Libido*. New York: International Universities Press.

Frattaroli, E. J. (1990). A new look at Hamlet: aesthetic response and Shakespeare's meaning. *International Review of Psycho-Analysis*, 17: 269–285.

Freud, S. (1900a). *The Interpretation of Dreams*. London: Pelican Freud Library, volume 4.

Freud, S. (1907a). Delusions and dreams in Jensen's *Gradiva*. *S.E.*, 9: 3–95. London: Hogarth.

Freud, S. (1908c). On the sexual theories of children. *S.E.*, 9: 207–226. London: Hogarth.

Freud, S. (1908d). "Civilized" sexual morality and modern nervous illness. *S.E.*, 9: 179–204. London: Hogarth.

Freud, S. (1911b). Formulation on the two principles of mental functioning. *S.E.*, 12: 213–226. London: Hogarth.

Freud, S. (1913f). The theme of the three caskets. *S.E.*, 12: 289–302. London: Hogarth.

Freud, S (1912–1913). *Totem and Taboo. S.E.*, 13: 1–161. London: Hogarth.

Freud S. (1914b). *The Moses of Michelangelo. S.E., 13*: 211–238. London: Hogarth.

Freud, S. (1914c). On narcissism: an introduction. *S.E., 14*: 67–102. London: Hogarth.

Freud, S. (1916d). Some character-types encountered in psychoanalytic work. *S.E., 14*: 309–334. London: Hogarth.

Freud, S. (1921c). *Group Psychology and the Analysis of the Ego. S.E., 18*: 65–144. London: Hogarth.

Freud, S. (1924). *Collected Papers.* London: Hogarth, volume 2.

Freud, S. (1925d). An autobiographical study. *S.E., 20*: 3–70. London: Hogarth.

Freud, S. (1925j). Some psychical consequences of the anatomical distinction between the sexes. *S.E., 19*: 243–258. London: Hogarth.

Freud, S. (1927d). Humour. *Standard Edition, 21*, 159–166. London: Hogarth.

Freud, S. (1933a). *New Introductory Lectures on Psychoanalysis. S.E., 22*: 3–182. London: Hogarth.

Freud, S., & J. Breuer (1895d). *Studies on Hysteria. S.E., 2.* London: Hogarth.

Gay, (1988). *Freud: A Life for Our Time.* London: Dent and Sons.

Gilligan, C. (1982). *In a Different Voice.* Cambridge, MA: Harvard University Press.

Gordon, H., Oyebode, O., & Minne, C. (1997). Death by homicide in special hospitals. *Journal of Forensic Psychiatry, 8*, 602-619.

Greenberg, B., & Rothenberg, A. (1974). William Shakespeare (1564–1616). Medico-psychological and psychoanalytic studies on his life and works: a bibliography. *International Review of Psycho-Analysis, 1*: 245–254.

Hall, P. (1982). Interview with John Russell Brown. In: J. R. Brown (Ed.), *Focus on Macbeth* (pp. 8–35). London: Routledge & Kegan Paul

Hanly, C. (1986). Lear and his daughters. *International Review of Psycho-Analysis, 13*: 211–220.

Henry IV, Part 1 (1989). Directed by David Giles, with Anthony Quayle, David Gwillim. London: BBC Enterprises Ltd.

Henry V (1989). Directed by Kenneth Branagh. Renaissance Films. DVD 9027619.

Hildebrand, H. P. (2006). The Caledonian tragedy. In: I. Wise and M. Mills (Eds.), *Psychoanalytic Ideas and Shakespeare* (pp. 43–63). London: Karnac.

Huggett, R. (1981). *The Curse of Macbeth and Other Theatrical Superstitions.* Oxford: Amber Lane Press.

Holland, N. N. (1968). Caliban's dream. *Psychoanalytic Quarterly, 37*: 114–125.

Holm, I. (n.d.). http://www.pbs.org/wgbh/masterpiece/archive/programs/kinglear/holm.html (accessed April 2006).

Jacobs, M. (1991a). *Insight and Experience: A Manual of Training in the Technique and Theory of Psychodynamic Counselling and Therapy.* Buckingham: Open University Press.

Jacobs, M. (1991b). The therapist's revenge: the law of talion as a motive for caring. *Contact — Interdisciplinary Journal of Pastoral Studies, 2: 105*, 2–11.

Jacobs, M. (2006). *The Presenting Past: the Core of Psychodynamic Counselling and Therapy* (3rd edn). Maidenhead: Open University Press.

Jekels, L. (1933). The problem of the duplicated expression of psychic themes. *International Journal of Psychoanalysis, 14*: 300–309.

Jones, E. (1918). Anal–erotic character traits. In: E. Jones (1961), *Papers on Psychoanalysis* (pp. 413–437). Boston: Beacon Press.

Jones, E. (1949). *Hamlet and Oedipus.* London: Gollancz.

King Lear (2006). Directed by Richard Eyre, with Ian Holm. DVD: ASIN: B000CZ0O3Q.

Kingham, M., & Gordon, H. (2004). Aspects of morbid jealousy. *Advances in Psychiatric Treatment, 10: 207–215.*

Kohlberg, L. (1981). *The Philosophy of Moral Development.* San Francisco, CA: Harper and Row.

Knights, L. C. (1964). How many children had Lady Macbeth? In: *Explorations* (pp.15–54). NewYork: New York University Press.

Kris, E. (1948). Prince Hal's conflict. *Psychoanalytic Quarterly, 17*: 487–506.

Krohn, J. (1986). The dangers of love in Antony and Cleopatra. *International Review of Psycho-Analysis, 13*: 89–96.

Levey, C. (1993). A bibliography of psychological and psychoanalytical Shakespeare criticism: 1979–89. In: B. J. Sokol (Ed.), *The Undiscover'd Country: New Essays on Psychoanalysis and Shakespeare* (pp. 217–248). London: Free Association.

Lichtenberg, J. D., & Lichtenberg, C. (1969). Prince Hal's conflict, adolescent idealism, and buffoonery. *Journal of the American Psychoanalytic Association, 17*: 873–887.

Lichtenberg, J. D., & Pao, P. (1974). Delusion, fantasy and desire. *International Journal of Psychoanalysis, 55*: 273–281.

Macbeth (1978). The Royal Shakespeare Company, directed by Trevor Nunn, with Ian McKellen and Judi Dench. DVD: FHED1776.

Macbeth (2001). The Royal Shakespeare Company, directed by Gregory Doran, with Antony Sher and Harriet Walter. DVD: Illuminations, www.illumin.co.uk.

Mahon, E. J. (1989). A note on "The theme of the three caskets". *Psychoanalytic Study of the Child, 44*: 325–330.

Masson, J. (Ed.) (1985). *The Complete Letters of Sigmund Freud to Wilhelm Fliess 1887–1904*. Cambridge, MA: Belknap.

Marazziti, D., Di Nasso, E., & Masala, I. (2003). Normal and obsessional jealousy: a study of a population of young adults. *European Psychiatry, 18,* 106-111.

Meisel, P., & Kendrick, W. (1985). *Bloomsbury/Freud: The Letters of James and Alix Strachey, 1924–1925*. New York: Basic Books.

Miller, J. (1993). *King Lear* in rehearsal. In: B. J. Sokol (Ed.) *The Undiscover'd Country: New Essays on Psychoanalysis and Shakespeare*. London: Free Association Books.

Moloney, J. C., & Rockelein, J. (1949). A new interpretation of Hamlet. *International Journal of Psychoanalysis, 30*: 92–106.

Muecke, D. C. (1969). *The Compass of Irony*. London: Methuen.

Murray, P. (1996). *Shakespeare's Imagined Persons: the Psychology of Role-Playing and Acting*. London: Macmillan.

Muslin, H. L. (1981). King Lear: images of the self in old age. *Journal of Mental Imagery, 5*: 143–156.

Muslin, H. L. (1988). *Macbeth. Psychoanalytic Psychotherapy, 5*: 357–368.

Oberndorf, C. P. (1934). Folie à deux. *International Journal of Psychoanalysis, 15*: 14–24.

Othello (2003). The Royal Shakespeare Company, directed by Trevor Nunn, with Willard White, Ian McKellen and Imogen Stubbs. DVD: B0000BZNJT.

Pao, P. (1968). On manic-depressive psychosis—a study of the transition of states. *Journal of the American Psychoanalytic Association, 16*: 809–831.

Paparo, F. (1984). Shakespeare's King Lear. *Annual Review of Psychoanalysis, 12*: 379–393.

Prospero's Books (1991). Directed by Peter Greenaway, with John Gielgud, and Michael. Guild Home Video: PUC 2199R.

Sachs, H. (1923). *The Tempest. International Journal of Psychoanalysis, 4*: 43–88.

Schücking, L. (1922). *Character Problems in Shakespeare's Plays*. London: Harrap.

Shapiro, J. (2005). *1599*. London: Faber and Faber.

Sharpe, E. F. (1946). From *King Lear* to *The Tempest*. *International Journal of Psychoanalysis, 27*: 19–30.

Shepherd, M. (1961). Morbid jealousy: some clinical and social aspects of a psychiatric symptom. *Journal of Mental Science, 107*: 688–704.

Simon, B. (1988). *Tragic Drama and the Family. Psychoanalytic Studies from Aeschylus to Beckett*. New Haven, CT: Yale University Press.

Sokol, B. J. (1993). *The Tempest*, "All torment, trouble, wonder and amazement": a Kleinian reading. In: B. J. Sokol (Ed.) *The Undiscover'd Country: New Essays in Psychoanalysis and Shakespeare* (pp. 179–216). London: Free Association.

Sokol, B. J. (1995). Constitutive signifiers or fetishes in Shakespeare's *The Merchant Of Venice*? *International Journal of Psychoanalysis, 76*: 373–387.

Stein, M. H. (1985). Irony in psychoanalysis. *Journal of the American Psychoanalytic Association, 33*: 35–57.

Stephens, L. (1993). A wilderness of monkeys: a psychodynamic study of *The Merchant of Venice*. In: B. J. Sokol (Ed.), *The Undiscover'd Country: New Essays on Psychoanalysis and Shakespeare* (pp. 91–129). London: Free Association Books.

Sterba, R. F. (1978). Discussions of Sigmund Freud. *Psychoanalytic Quarterly, 47*: 173–191.

Stewart, J. I. M. (1949). *Character and Motive in Shakespeare*. London: Longman.

Stoppard, T. (1990). *Rosencrantz and Guildenstern Are Dead*. Second Sight Films: 2N DVD 3021.

Symons, N. J. (1928). The graveyard scene in *Hamlet*. *International Journal of Psychoanalysis, 9*: 6–119.

The Merchant of Venice (1992). Directed by Jonathan Miller, with Laurence Olivier and Joan Plowright. Polygram 083 3943.

The Merchant of Venice (2000). Directed by Trevor Nunn, with Henry Goodman. The Performance Company: MTD 5123.

The Tempest (1979). Directed by Derek Jarman. Second Sight Films: 2NDVD 3056.

The Winter's Tale (1999). Directed by Greg Doran. A Heritage Theatre Digital Video Production. London: Heritage Theatre Ltd. DVD: B0000BZNJT.

Todd, J., & Dewhurst, K. (1955). The Othello Syndrome, a study in the psychopathology of sexual jealousy. *Journal of Nervous and Mental Disease, 122*: 367–374.

Waelder, R. (1930). The principle of multiple function: observations on overdetermination. In: S. Guttman (Ed.), *Psychoanalysis: Observation, Theory, Application* (pp. 248–274). New York: International Universities Press, 1976.

Wangh, M. (1950). Othello: The tragedy of Iago. *Psychoanalytic Quarterly, 19*: 202–212.

Welldon, E. (1988). *Mother, Madonna, Whore.* London: Free Association Books.

Wells, S., & Taylor, G. (1987). *The Complete Oxford Shakespeare.* Oxford: Oxford University Press.

West, L. J. (1968). The Othello syndrome. *Contemporary Psychoanalysis, 4*: 103–110.

Willbern, D. (1978). William Shakespeare: a bibliography of psychoanalytic and psychological criticism, 1964–1975. *International Review of Psycho-Analysis, 5*: 361–371.

Wilson, J. Dover (1944). *The Fortunes of Falstaff.* Cambridge: Cambridge University Press.

Winnicott, D. W. (1971). *Playing and Reality.* London: Routledge.

INDEX